"Whether you've been intrigued with the Amish for a lifetime or are just curious, you'll be sure to enjoy *Amish Weddings*. Prepare yourself to be surprised and intrigued as future couples embark on their first date, then their marital ceremony, followed by a joyous party including a sumptuous, mouthwatering meal. Author Beth Oberholtzer has done thorough research and writes in an entertaining fashion that kept me enthralled. Lovely illustrations, too!"

—**KATE LLOYD**, bestselling author of the Legacy of Lancaster Trilogy, the Lancaster Discoveries series, *A Lancaster Family Christmas*, and *A Lancaster Family Secret*

"Sensitive, revealing, and filled with the voices of real people, *Amish Weddings* is a fascinating exploration of these community and family celebrations. As she unpacks the customs and traditions around courtship, marriage, and singleness, Beth Oberholtzer explains not only Amish weddings but a great deal about Amish culture more broadly. The outstanding photos add another dimension to this important book."

—**STEVEN M. NOLT**, director of the Young Center for Anabaptist and Pietists Studies at Elizabethtown College

"Having attended many Amish weddings, I can attest that Beth Oberholtzer's *Amish Weddings* captures the essence of these beautiful and unique events perfectly. Her detailed research and respectful portrayal bring to life the authenticity and deep community spirit that define Amish celebrations. This book is an invaluable window into a world of love, tradition, and unwavering faith."

—**SUSAN HOUGELMAN**, owner and operator of Simple Life Tours and author of *Inside the Simple Life: Finding Inspiration among the Amish*

"This book is equal parts delightful and detailed. You'll learn everything you might want to know about how an Amish wedding happens."

—**ERIK WESNER**, founder and editor of AmishAmerica.com

"Are you curious about Amish courtship, weddings, and the early days of married life? *Amish Weddings* by Beth Oberholtzer provides a detailed and captivating look into these unique traditions from Lancaster, Pennsylvania, enriched with real-life testimonies. It is a must-read for anyone interested in Amish culture."

—**JOE KEIM**, author of *My People, the Amish: The True Story of an Amish Father and Son*

Amish Weddings
From Courtship to Celebration

Amish Weddings

From Courtship to Celebration

BETH OBERHOLTZER

HERALD PRESS

Harrisonburg, Virginia

To those who seek to act justly and to love mercy and to walk humbly with their God.

DOUG HOOVER

Herald Press
PO Box 866, Harrisonburg, Virginia 22803
www.HeraldPress.com

Library of Congress Cataloging-in-Publication Data
Names: Oberholtzer, Beth author
Title: Amish weddings : from courtship to celebration / Beth Oberholtzer.
Description: Harrisonburg, Virginia : Herald Press, [2024] | Includes
    bibliographical references.
Identifiers: LCCN 2024034399 | ISBN 9781513813615 hardcover
Subjects: LCSH: Amish—Marriage customs and rites—Pennsylvania—Lancaster
    County | Amish—Pennsylvania—Lancaster County—Social life and customs
    | Weddings—Pennsylvania—Lancaster County |
    Courtship—Pennsylvania—Lancaster County
Classification: LCC F157.L2 O24 2024 | DDC
    974.8150088287—dc23/eng/20241011
LC record available at https://lccn.loc.gov/2024034399

AMISH WEDDINGS
© 2025 by Herald Press, Harrisonburg, Virginia 22803. 800-245-7894.
All rights reserved.
Library of Congress Control Number: 2024034399
International Standard Book Number: 978-1-5138-1361-5
Printed in United States of America
Cover design by Merrill Miller. Interior design by Beth Oberholtzer and Merrill Miller.
Cover photo by Christy Kauffman.
Back cover photos, top to bottom: John Herr, Christy Kauffman, Beth Oberholtzer.
Author photo by Luis Raul, TRPhotography.co.

29 28 27 26 25   10 9 8 7 6 5 4 3 2 1

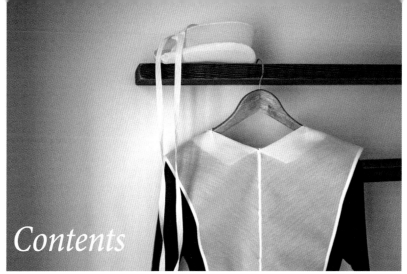

CHRISTY KAUFFMAN

Contents

Foreword

JOHN HERR

A wedding that recently went viral on social media featured two young men hired as wedding attendants. They danced their way down the aisle with incredible flair, delighting the guests with their unexpected and impressive performance.

Their dance clearly entertained, but it left me with a pit in my stomach. Entertainment at a reception is one thing, but during the sacred ceremony itself? It felt distracting, irreverent, even flippant.

The Plain people have a completely different approach to weddings. Their ceremonies are still joyful, but they stick to a well-worn tradition. They focus on gathering the community to witness the solemn exchange of vows. While there might be some small personal touches, like little take-home gifts for the guests, there's a comforting sameness to each wedding.

That's the big difference between Plain weddings and, well, not-Plain weddings. In English (as us non-Amish are called) weddings, there's often a focus on being unique, individual, and unforgettable. The dancing attendants at that wedding definitely left an impression, but will the guests remember much else? What about the couple, the weightiness of their vows?

And that's what I think gets lost sometimes in these non-Plain weddings—the vows. The traditions in Plain weddings emphasize the sacredness of the promises made between the couple before God. Those vows are what should take our breath away, not the entertainment that surrounds them.

You'll get a sense of that in *Amish Weddings* by Beth Oberholtzer. This lovely book offers a rare and beautiful glimpse into the heart of Plain wedding traditions. With stunning photography that takes you right into Lancaster County, Pennsylvania, the book shows the careful preparations that go into these special days. The vignettes and recipes included add a touch of the simple life that's so appealing.

But what really makes this book special is how it reminds us of what truly matters. It's not about trying to "go Amish," but about reflecting on what's important in our own lives. In a world where we often get caught up in the flashy and the forgettable, *Amish Weddings* encourages us to hold on to what's dear and to cherish those sacred moments. It's a lovely reminder to appreciate the traditions that bring us together. To focus on the love and promises that truly matter—like wedding vows that take our breath away.

> —*Suzanne Woods Fisher, bestselling, award-winning author of over forty books, fiction and nonfiction, many of which are about the Old Order Amish. Her grandfather was raised Plain in Franklin County, Pennsylvania.*

Preface

As a native and current resident of Lancaster County, Pennsylvania, home to a large Amish population, I'm fortunate to have developed relationships with Amish friends who have shared with me about their horses, mules, and gardens when I researched previous books. When I started asking questions for this book about youth groups and weddings that one friend couldn't answer, she directed me to a well-known Amish historian. At the end of the route, I drove down a lane toward a multigeneration farmhouse and stopped in front of a barn. The historian, in his late seventies, was at the open door repairing a piece of furniture. He was immediately gracious and hauled two chairs out to the yard so we could sit down and chat. We talked about weddings and my intentions for this book. He answered my questions, told stories, and sketched little illustrations on one of my tablet pages.

Our conversation naturally turned toward Amish people I met related to my other books whom he also knew. I asked how, with the many thousands of Amish in Lancaster County, I kept meeting people who knew each other. His response: "I guess the good Lord leads you to them."

As I researched this book, people were generally happy to talk with me about their wedding experiences and memories. When I pressed for specific wording to describe customs and events, I realized that I was asking for details that they needed to translate in their heads from Pennsylvania

German to English before relaying the information to me. All Amish likely know a certain amount of High German and are fluent in English, but their native language is Pennsylvania German (often called Pennsylvania Dutch), a spoken rather than written dialect. In some cases, different words were used to describe the same thing. For example, the four young people who attend the bride and groom on the wedding day might be called side sitters, *Newesitzer*, attendants, or witnesses.

One Amish man in his thirties suggested a different title for this book when I talked to him as he mashed potatoes for an Amish wedding feast fundraiser; he thought it should be "Organized Chaos." This general sentiment was suggested, with a hint of apology, by many others. But *organized* is the operative word here. What might look random on the surface has a strong underlying structure. A good bit of that structure has to do with the way the Amish are categorized and categorize themselves throughout life, mostly according to gender and age. They are male or female; they are of a certain age; they are single, or dating, or engaged, or married. They often have young children or children who are old enough to run around, or their children have grown up and gotten married and have their own youngsters. Though rare, perhaps a grown child has left the church. People are quicker to define themselves related to their families and church districts rather than by how they earn a living.

The customs and rituals described in *Amish Weddings* are distinctive to the Old Order Amish in Lancaster County and its daughter settlements outside the county, which maintain close ties to Lancaster County. There are other Amish-related groups in Lancaster County and Old Order Amish in other areas that have practices different from those noted here. What I describe in this book reflects the traditions and experiences of those I interviewed; certainly a community as large as the Lancaster County Amish will have variations large and small. Though it's easy to view the Amish as frozen in time, they are constantly growing and evolving even as they stay true to their faith, their families, and their community.

Weddings are private affairs of great religious significance that are not open to outside visitors. The Amish in general do not allow photos to be taken of them. Thus, many photos in this book are of things rather than people. Permission was given by those who appeared in some way in the photos or owned the items shown. Throughout the book, I quote various individuals and recount their stories. All names have been changed, but the voices are genuine.

Though the marriage ceremony in the morning is solemn, the rest of the wedding day is filled with a swirl of action, talking, and laughter. Church friends and buddies and family members visit with one another. Young people reconnect or make new friends; they talk, play games, and gather to sing. Workers are in constant motion, whether cooking, serving, or ushering people to the table for more food. No more welcome words were spoken than those from a *Forgeher* (usher) when I was a guest: "Someone will come find you when it's time to eat."

* * * *

I am grateful for the willingness of the more than seventy members of the Lancaster County Old Order Amish community who allowed me to visit with them. Many met with me multiple times and answered my random questions with grace. They told me stories and sent me to others for additional information. Several business and shop owners provided their professional insights.

Each subject in the book was discussed with multiple people who provided varying perspectives that were incorporated into the narrative. More than a dozen Amish readers gave feedback on the whole book before its publication. Among them: two bishops, a minister, a historian, mothers, grandmothers and great-grandmothers, parents of married sons and daughters, recently married couples, and an author of wedding and homemaker planning books.

Chef Tim Ardinger lent his expertise by interviewing cooks, researching foodways, and fine-tuning recipes.

The historian I spoke with had very specific instructions on what this book should be. "It should be factual, pleasing to read, and make sense." I have done my best to make it so.

ONE

Introduction to Amish Weddings

Families often live in connected or adjacent dwellings on the same property or farm. BETH OBERHOLTZER

Amish weddings in Lancaster County are daylong celebrations, a blend of church and community, the sacred and the earthly. An hours-long morning church service culminates in a brief wedding ceremony. After a noon meal for hundreds, the newly married couple and guests enjoy singing, snacking, and playing games. It is a wonderful opportunity to catch up with family and friends. Teasing and lighthearted pranks are often a part of the day.

While older guests and families with young children may head home in the late afternoon, the family and young people stay on for supper, more visiting, and singing—sometimes late into the evening.

The route to marriage does not begin with the dramatic presentation of a ring answered by exclamations of delight. It begins with a life cocooned by family, in a place of belonging where parents, friends, relatives, and siblings show the way. The youngest daughter in a family may be separated from her oldest sister by eight siblings and twelve or more years. As she grows up she sees her brothers and sisters socialize with friends and begin dating in the same way she can anticipate doing herself. Her brothers come to understand the importance of their leadership and partnership in both dating and in the work to make a wedding. Stories from her parents and grandparents about their weddings carry a familiar pattern.

Amish weddings are an affirmation of the importance of relationships—of the family unit, of the church community, and of an abiding faith in God. There are no rings or fancy gowns, no photographers or dance bands. The bride and groom must be members of the Amish church before marriage, as directed in 2 Corinthians 6:14, "Be ye not unequally yoked together with unbelievers."

Each bride and groom are unique in their personalities and their care for each other. But they are also an integral part of a larger whole, surrounded by family and friends who welcome their joining as important to maintaining tradition. Great joy is found by all when a new family unit is formed, and the addition of children is happily anticipated, a continuation of faith and the community.

Deep Roots

Ancestors of the present-day Amish left Europe in the 1700s seeking freedom from religious persecution and access to good farmland. They and their fellow Anabaptists, the Mennonites, were offered both by Pennsylvania founder William Penn. As Anabaptists, the Amish believe in voluntary church membership and adult baptism. They seek to follow the teachings of Jesus daily by valuing modesty and humility and living peaceably with others and in opposition to conflict and war. Their loyalty is not to any government on this earth but to the kingdom of God.

Their deep commitment to maintaining separation from the world is carried out in both the religious and practical realms. The "Old Order" in their name signifies the maintenance of traditional ways, including traveling by horse-drawn carriage, farming with mules or draft horses instead of tractors, functioning without electricity, and strictly limiting the use of telephones.

Amish women find ways to add a touch of whimsy in the garden and celebrate their families at the same time. Parents often make and display visual representations of their family members in their homes, perhaps on a series of hanging small wooden plaques. Dad's and Mom's names appear at the top, with the names of their children and their birthdays below. When a child marries, the spouse's name is added, as are the names of any subsequent grandchildren. **TOP:** DON SHENK, **LEFT:** BETH OBERHOLTZER

Worship in Homes

An Amish church is a body of believers, not the building where they meet. Following a centuries-long tradition, the Amish meet in homes—or shops or outbuildings—rather than church buildings for Sunday worship.

Members of the Old Order Amish church meet within geographically defined districts. Each district is made up of thirty to forty families and is typically led by a bishop, two or three ministers, and a deacon; a bishop may oversee more than one church. District services are held every other Sunday. Weddings, which are largely church services, are held at the home of the bride.

Just as in many other faith traditions, an Amish wedding is performed at a house of worship and incorporates elements of a church service. But the comparison is tenuous. Amish weddings take place at the home of the bride—which also serves on a rotating basis as a house of worship for the church district—and includes a three-hour worship service. The ceremony and meal may take place in the house itself, in an outbuilding of some sort, or in a specially constructed or rented wedding house.

Traditionally, Amish weddings took place after the fall harvest, between mid-October and early December—always on a Tuesday or Thursday. With a growing Amish population in Lancaster County, some communities were blessed with eight or ten weddings in one day; it was difficult for ministers to keep up and for invitees to split their loyalties. Since off-farm work schedules are no longer dictated by the vagaries of weather and seasons, spring—from January through March—has become an acceptable part of the wedding season as well.

A massive amount of volunteer labor is necessary to stage a wedding. Since Sundays are a day of rest, a Tuesday wedding can be prepared for on Monday and cleaned up after on Wednesday; furnishings for a Thursday wedding can be set up on Wednesday and torn down on Friday.

A family may attend more than ten weddings in one season, occasionally two in one day. An outsider may question how a worker can take off in the middle of the work week—once and sometimes twice a week over several months—to attend weddings. Amish workers typically have more autonomy than other workers; they may be self-employed, work for an Amish-owned business, or have non-Amish coworkers who can maintain the business when they're out. In any case, the Amish are known to be hard workers and make up for what they miss by routinely working on federal holidays and working extra on evenings and Saturdays.

An immediately obvious difference between an Amish wedding and an English (as the non-Amish are called) wedding involves numbers and volume. When a family includes eight or more siblings and thirty aunts and uncles, the number of cousins can easily reach a hundred or more. Add in youth group friends and the thirty or more families that are part of the bride's church, and it doesn't take long to total hundreds who will share in the big day. And hundreds of people gathering over a daylong celebration expect to eat. Fortunately, many who attend the wedding lend a willing hand to make it possible.

Amish weddings traditionally take place in the fall after the crops are harvested. Each year, many couples marry, so the wedding season has expanded into the spring. CHRISTY KAUFFMAN

The bride's side of the family does the bulk of the preparation before the wedding and performs myriad duties on the wedding day itself. Immediate family members, close friends, aunts and uncles, neighbors, and fellow church members are honored to do their part for the couple as they help "make a wedding."

Elizabeth's grandson got married last year. She easily listed how weddings today are the same as her wedding over sixty years ago: songs, preaching, side sitters (attendants), dinner menu, Eck tenders (couples who serve the bride and groom while they are seated at the corner, or *Eck* in Pennsylvania German, of the dining table and throughout the day). What has changed? "There are more guests, and the young people play volleyball in the afternoon."

Though the particulars that define Amish weddings remain—a morning church service, the dinner menu, the day's schedule, and the gathering hosted by the bride's family—some traditions do change over time.

- Wedding plans are not usually considered a secret—as in previous generations—and can be discussed prior to being published, when an upcoming marriage is formally announced to the church (which takes place a few weeks before the wedding). As the Lancaster County Amish *Gemeinschaft* (community) continues to settle more broadly outside of the county, relatives need earlier notice so they can make travel plans.

- Brides, supported by their side sitters, Eck tenders, and buddies, are likely to express more of their personality when choosing dress colors, table decorations, special foods and beverages, and the snack and supper menus.

- The couple receives and opens more gifts at the wedding itself than in the past; however, they still make post-wedding visits and accept gifts then.

- Not as many pranks are played on the wedding day, but many grooms still get tossed over fences.

- Unmarried couples may be paired in rows when they go in to sing on the afternoon of the wedding day, rather than girls waiting for boys to ask them individually.

An Amish wedding cannot be discussed without exploring what leads a couple to marry. The following chapters take the reader through the process, from young people socializing in youth groups to couples meeting and dating to their engagement and preparation for the wedding, and then finally the day itself.

Prior to marriage, Amish youth participate in one of a wide web of youth groups. Amish youth groups are kind of like social clubs; they provide space and time for young people in their upper teens and twenties to see friends within a supervised framework. They play games, share meals, and sing at their Sunday get-togethers. Often within this group, or adjacent to the group, a young man notices a young woman and asks her out. If she says yes, they begin dating regularly. Families get to know each other. Parents and friends keep a close eye on things. Maybe there will be a wedding!

TWO

Amish Youth

Many a young man or woman enjoys driving their horse while it pulls a one-seat sulky. DOUG HOOVER

An Amish child's life is centered on family and home. In addition to children playing with siblings, a family's social life might largely consist of visiting relatives and friends. All attend biweekly church services held in members' homes, followed by a noon meal and visiting time. A family highlight might be going on a trip to see relatives in another state.

Teen life

While their English counterparts are attending high school and perhaps college, Amish teens are making significant progress toward becoming adults. They are taking on increased responsibilities within and outside of the family. Since schooling ends at age fifteen, a large part of a young person's time and energy after that point goes toward work. Each gradually learns how to handle their own finances. A young man explores jobs that will lead to supporting a family while a young woman often finds work in the service realm.

Several significant events serve as markers as young people mature. At sixteen, Amish girls and boys join a youth group and socialize weekly with other young people. A majority of Amish youth are baptized into the church in their late teens or early twenties. Baptism is one of the most important rituals in the Amish faith, signifying a lifetime commitment to God and to the church community.

Farewell to school days

Amish children learn their lessons in private one-room schoolhouses that are within walking—or scootering—distance of their homes. Formal education beyond eighth grade isn't seen as necessary, since the Amish typically support themselves through farming and trades that are taught on the job through informal apprenticeships. There is also the concern that further schooling pulls an individual away from the community and introduces ideas that are not consistent with their Christian values.

Since Pennsylvania requires school attendance for Amish students up to age fifteen, those who are still fourteen at the completion of eighth grade attend an Amish-organized "vocational school" for three hours once a week until they turn fifteen. Teachers help students review some of their eighth-grade lessons and check on the students' workweek accomplishments. Teaching focuses on arithmetic, which is vital to working in business and handling household finances, and German vocabulary, which leads to greater understanding of the German used throughout Sunday services in Scripture readings, hymns, and sermons. And there are often spirited games of volleyball at break time.

Jobs then and now

When families lived almost exclusively on farms, work for an Amish girl meant helping her mother in the house by caring for younger siblings, gardening, preserving food, cooking, and cleaning—and perhaps helping in the fields. An Amish boy helped his father on the farm. Depending on the age of her siblings and how much she was needed at home, a girl of fourteen might have gone out each day to help a relative or fellow farm family care for their young children and do housework. A boy might have worked on a neighboring farm.

A teen girl today still helps at home but has additional employment choices. She may work in a market or in a restaurant or she may clean houses. Many young women enjoy volunteering as side-walkers at an Amish-owned therapeutic equine riding center.

Community and school leadership may recognize a young Amish woman's potential when she is between seventeen and twenty and invite her to become a schoolteacher. Teachers in Amish schools have completed their Amish schooling but have not gone beyond that. To learn the job, they participate in teacher meetings, study resources, review the curriculum, and often help in the classroom. A teacher will generally stay on the job until she gets married and sometimes longer.

If a young man is not engaged in farming, he might join his father's on-farm or nearby commercial business or work "away from home." Thriving local communities offer jobs in agriculture services, in building or construction, in shops, or with foodstuffs. In jobs unique to the Old Order community, a young man might work as a farmhand, learn to shoe horses, or train in a carriage-building shop.

Reuben is an eighteen-year-old Amish man; his brother, who is a few years older, recently got married and would be taking over the family farm.

Since her family will be hosting youth group on Sunday, Mary mows the meadow to prepare it for volleyball. JOHN HERR

Reuben had been his dad's farmhand, but he had started working away as a carpenter. But he didn't want carpentering for his "married job." In his heart he's a farmer. One older brother farmed produce, another worked away part-time and farmed a bit. Farmland in Lancaster County is dear—whether buying or renting—but Reuben's family might be able to help when the time came. Amish farmers often move to the less populated areas of the county or into other counties or states in search of affordable farmland.

The money that young people earn doing work outside of the home is routinely passed along to their parents. A small portion may be handed back as spending money. Teens live in the family home with their expenses covered the same as when they were younger. When they reach twenty or twenty-one, the money they earn becomes theirs alone. The family generally works as a team to make decisions; young people clearly value the counsel of their elders.

Dad and Mom advise on (and likely finance) the purchase of a carriage horse when their son is between sixteen and eighteen. A horse that

A young man values an attractive and spirited horse. His harness and carriage might show a bit more pizzazz than an older married man would display. JOHN HERR

handles easily is vital for safety, but good looks are appreciated too. Young women generally use the family horse and carriage when needed.

At the same time a young man is looking at horses, he's thinking about his carriage. He'll likely outfit the inside with plush carpet and a polished wooden dashboard that includes light switches, and a fancier speedometer and clock than an older man would find necessary. His horse's bridle and backstrap might be embellished with color blocks, and the harness padding might sport a color that contrasts with the black harness. He might add battery-operated purple glow lights under the buggy to subtly light the night. There may be more safety reflectors on the back than are strictly necessary. These little pushes against the ordinary allow a bit of individuality without compromising the important tenets of one's faith.

The Amish are greatly admired for their dedication to hard work. Time with family and friends often involves doing something useful. Extended family and neighbors help one another harvest hay and corn. Men—young and old—show up with their toolbelts when help with a building project is needed, and the women prepare meals for the laborers. Several generations of women often have "parties" throughout the summer preparing fresh garden produce to be preserved. The inclination to work hard is instilled in children and teens through custom and experience.

Travel for the greater good

A popular way for young people to both help others and socialize is by going on out-of-state service trips to aid in disaster recovery. Storm Aid, an Amish-run organization under the umbrella of Mennonite Disaster Service, selects a site each year in an area where homes have been damaged because of a natural disaster. Each season, from October through May, more than 550 young Amish women and men are bused from Lancaster County to work for a week or more at a time repairing and rebuilding.[1] Many others volunteer annually through CARE (Community Aid Relief Effort), an Amish-directed agency, for two-week stints. They believe that it is important to "let your light so shine before men, that they may see your good works, and glorify your Father which is in heaven" (Matthew 5:16).

These trips allow young workers to follow the Christian mandate of serving others while learning about different communities, spending time with friends, and making new ones. After a day of cleanup, painting, and construction, youth enjoy visiting together—and often do a bit of sightseeing after their week of work.

Changing clothes

Turning sixteen is a big step toward adulthood for Amish youth. Though not immediately obvious to the outside observer, wardrobe changes mark the new maturity. Boys from toddler age to age fifteen wear a Sunday suit that includes a boxy jacket with a high rounded neck called a *Vammes*. At sixteen, a boy switches to a more tailored style called a *Mutse* that features a collarless deep V at the front and a pieced back with a single vent.

He will likely also switch to a church hat with a three-inch brim. Young men at sixteen in some communities elect not to wear hats for work or casual socializing, but they will begin wearing hats for those occasions again when they get married. In other communities, young men wear hats when socializing and at work throughout their youth.

Girls continue to wear the same dress styles when they turn sixteen as they have previously. As they mature and likely begin making their own dresses, they may have a little more freedom to pick the exact fabric and color they prefer. Small variations over the years or within a social set might relate to length of the skirt, drop of the waist, or fit of the sleeves.

Committing to God and the community

Choosing to receive baptism into the Amish church is the most important decision a young person can make. It is a lifetime commitment to God and to following the biblical teachings of Jesus. And it is an agreement to follow the *Ordnung*, or code of conduct, of the community (*Ordnung* means "order" in German; in Amish communities, these guidelines govern personal and communal practice). The Amish, as Anabaptists, believe in voluntary church membership and adult baptism.

Since Amish churches hold baptism services for a class (group of candidates) every two years, a young person gives careful thought about the best time to join. They want to be sure of both the decision and the timing. In some youth groups, baptism is necessary before an individual may begin dating, whereas in others the anticipation of marrying within the church might provide the incentive to join a baptism class, even if a young person is not yet dating.

Though it varies among groups, girls are usually sixteen or seventeen and boys eighteen or nineteen when they join the church. Within a district, there may be eight to ten in a class. After several months of biweekly instruction, the class takes the vows during a morning church service. Most young people raised in the Amish community join the church.

Socializing in youth groups

At sixteen, a young person's world broadens when they join one of the many youth groups open to them. This opportunity to mix with others their age and enjoy themselves without direct parental supervision is an exciting time. Each group consists of roughly sixty to ninety young Amish people who range in age from sixteen to their mid-twenties or older. Youth groups meet every Sunday from three or four in the afternoon until late in the evening; participants enjoy games, meals, socializing, and singing.

Amelia's First Attendance

Amelia could hardly contain herself. Finally, she had turned sixteen and could start attending youth group gatherings! Choosing which youth group to join had been relatively simple. Her two older brothers were both members of the Parakeets, and she could easily travel to Sunday get-togethers with them. Her cousin Elsie was also a member, as were two girls from her church, so she already knew some people.

Amelia's younger sister Roselyn couldn't believe how quickly their mother agreed that a new dress was warranted. Amelia chose a beautiful navy fabric to make her dress and cape to go under her black apron. (The new dress would be perfect for church, too, with a white cape and apron.) Her usual white covering, black stockings, and black leather church shoes completed the look.

One Saturday, Amelia washes the family carriage that she will drive to her youth group meeting on Sunday. Her at-home attire includes a kerchief head covering and a bib-style apron. BETH OBERHOLTZER

Amelia's first youth group meeting was more than twenty-five miles from their home a few miles southeast of Lancaster City—too far for their horse to travel in a single trip. So she and her brother set out early Sunday afternoon, driving their horse and carriage an hour south to Quarryville, where they met up with others and stabled their horse. The group of nine continued another hour and a half south to Nottingham in a spring wagon pulled by two horses. They arrived right around three in the afternoon and joined the eighty other youth at the host's farm.

Though Amelia was too nervous to immediately join in the volleyball game (she did play a bit of spikeball), the others welcomed her. By suppertime, she felt more at ease with the girls around her table and the boys at the neighboring table.

Selecting one's companions

Youth and their parents decide on an appropriate group for the young person, often selecting a group based on the group that siblings, cousins, friends from school, or friends from church have joined. They also take other factors into account.

- Level of supervision: Most youth groups are supervised, which means there is an advisory board of ministers and a leadership committee made up of parents. Roughly 60 percent of youth are part of supervised groups. They have twice-yearly meetings of all members, parents, and advisors to review the guidelines and to address issues that come up. Families and church communities may feel different levels of comfort with what is generally accepted within a group and may make decisions about which group they join related to that.

- Geography: Some groups have broad geographic parameters (such as "east of the county line, south of Elizabethtown, west of New Holland, and north of Route 30"), whereas others are open to all youth who are part of the Amish community who live within or not far outside the borders of Lancaster County.

- Sports: Though volleyball is an integral part of most youth group gatherings, some groups also play in outside tournaments—which may not be inviting to youth who are not quite such avid players. Parents may prefer their children enjoy baseball tournaments at members' farms rather than at municipal parks. Some may steer clear of baseball altogether and stick with volleyball. There is a recent interest in pickleball, which is sometimes even played at weddings.

After a youth group is selected, the decision is not written in stone. A move from one to another may be related to age or friendships. Those who are original to a group are called "beginners"; those added later are called "joiners." A young man may move to a group that includes a young woman whom he might be interested in dating. If a young woman's friends in a group marry young and she has not, she may look to a group that has a largely older cohort. This could be older girls with whom she can share a friendship or older boys she may be open to dating. One young man dropped out of a group because their baseball team often played local English teams on weeknights, and it was too hard to get up at five in the morning and go to his job pouring concrete.

Folks in their seventies and eighties recall just four or five youth groups open to them when they were in their late teens; in 2024, the numbers had grown to more than sixty-two hundred young people participating in over a hundred groups. Roughly three to five groups are added each year. This echoes the increase in the Old Order Amish population of Lancaster County, which grew from an estimated seven thousand in 1970 to over forty-four thousand in 2023.[2]

Families are still very much a part of a young person's experience. Parents support and stay connected with their children by hosting youth gatherings, and parents and siblings often attend youth group games and other special events.

When a group reaches a hundred or more young people, the size becomes unwieldy; it is difficult to get to know others, and hosting becomes a challenge. Leadership and youth make plans regarding how best to split, sometimes along geographic lines. Care is taken to maintain a mix of ages. Subsequent groups often maintain the original names, adding number or letter designations. For example, there are five groups with the name Robins, three named Ravens, and four Meadowlark subgroups. Directions, letters, or numbers may be added when groups split and both maintain the original name such as Robins NW. Groups also come up with their own names: Bird names are common (Wrens, Doves, Eagles, Hummingbirds, Hawks) as are wild animals (Tigers, Cougars, Cheetahs, Chipmunks), horse breeds (Morgans, Mustangs), historical or cultural figures (Pilgrims, Wranglers, Titans), and natural elements (Icebergs, Acorns).

The vocabulary pertaining to youth groups has changed, and variations continue depending on location and traditions. One young woman might ask her cousin, "Where is the hop this week?" Her parents might discuss what the "gang" will be doing, and her grandparents talk about "going to a singin." It's up to the youth to explain, "It's not a *gang* anymore, Mom!" or, "It's more than just singing, *Mammi* (Grandma)."

It may not seem flattering to be described as a "peanut butter," but it's an easy—if inexplicable—reference to a young person who is fourteen or fifteen, almost the age at which they can join a youth group. A peanut butter may participate in some youth-group-adjacent activities, such as filling in if a baseball team runs short of players. Roselyn, just fifteen, was pleased to be allowed to join in playing games when her sister's youth group met at their house.

Rumspringa years

Rumspringa literally translates to "running around." Though in popular culture it is thought to be a time for Amish young people to go wild before settling down and joining the church, for many communities in Lancaster County it is much tamer. "Running around" is a term that simply means socializing with friends. So Rumspringa is the time—age sixteen until marriage—that young people can socialize outside of the family and learn to know one another at regular get-togethers. Most maintain the *Ordnung* (rules and behavioral expectations) of their faith and have no desire to push the boundaries of acceptable behavior—at least not very far.

Before a young person joins the church, some of the offenses might involve use of cell phones—perhaps taking photos and trying out social media. Given the easy access, some Amish teens are known to have Facebook or Instagram accounts where they post and follow their friends. A more progressive youth group may turn a temporary blind eye, whereas a more traditional group might suspend the smartphone owner.

"Sometimes driving a truck gets in the way of joining the church."

Other likely temporary transgressions are easier to observe. Young men may drive cars, perhaps with young women as passengers. Both might dress "English" on occasion, and some boys get English haircuts. They might watch movies or listen to music. A step further might take them to bars or clubs.

Stories abound, particularly from the 1970s to 1990s, of groups of Amish youth behaving badly by drinking, dancing, and partying. Local police needed to contend with hundreds of young men in buggies gathered in small towns or public areas on Saturday evenings, some engaging in disruptive behavior that included racing in the streets. On occasion, the local police asked Amish church leadership to control their youth—or the police would need to step in.

A sobering wake-up call arrived in 1998. Two young Amish men were charged with distributing cocaine supplied by members of the Pagan motorcycle gang. They had sold or given cocaine and methamphetamine to other Amish youth at social gatherings. Stunned family members stood publicly with the young men, who immediately pled guilty and agreed to work for the police undercover. The two spoke at private gatherings all over Lancaster County warning Amish youth and parents about the dangers of drugs. Because the young men took immediate responsibility and had strong community support, they were each given a sentence of only one year in prison and five years of supervised release.

Voluntary supervision

With this and other misconduct in mind, concerned parents and ministers gathered in late 1998 to address how to tamp down the questionable

Youth in some areas may use a cell phone during their running-around years; however, in other areas, owning a phone could result in expulsion from youth group. Such infractions are confessed and remedied prior to marriage. DOUG HOOVER

behavior of some of the young people and offer support for those who wished for a stronger structure for their social gatherings. Several prominent church bishops offered assistance in writing guidelines for newly forming youth groups. The new rules outlined the expectations for "supervised" groups going forward: No Saturday evening gatherings; all activities for the Sunday gatherings would be at one location to cut down on large groups traveling from one place to another; singings would be from the *Ausbund* (Amish hymnal) and *Gesangbuch* ("songbook," also called the "brown book" or "thin book") within specific time frames; and all must leave by ten at night.[3]

All were committed to making the groups beneficial for the youth. Parents worked and planned with other parents and with their children, and church leadership provided support. They understood that youth sometimes make questionable choices, but a strong social framework can encourage good choices.

The idea of formal guidance quickly caught on. New groups formed one after the other, the Eagles followed by the Hummingbirds followed by the Parakeets—each tweaking the guideline details a bit, but all directed by advisory boards consisting of bishops and ministers and caretaker boards made up of parents.

By 2003 there were approximately six hundred Lancaster County Amish youth in supervised groups. Pleased parents worked to extend supervision to established groups.[4] Establishing guidelines clearly had a positive impact. Just over twenty-five years after their initial formation, the original three groups have grown so large that they each split and expanded into ten or more groups.

But what happens when someone steps outside of the lines? The original instructions outlined what would happen if a young person violated group guidelines. A series of escalating consequences—from visits by leadership to temporary exclusion from group participation to expulsion—were enacted.

Though this was the initial plan, reconciliation within youth groups in the several decades since has been fine-tuned based on circumstances and experience.

Some of the more conservative Amish districts may not find the change to "supervised" necessary; they may prefer to keep things as they were. Their youth may have jobs close to home that keep them well within the sphere of family and church. They are less likely to be in contact with some of the worldly influences than young people working in the broader community, and are thus less tempted to engage in illicit behavior.

Parents and other leadership of one of the more traditional supervised youth groups met one summer evening to discuss a few concerns. The issues may seem minor to some, but they illustrate the importance of separation from the wider world and the value of maintaining community.

- Some of the young men were "rowdy," stepping out and coming back in during the evening's singing.

- Young women were choosing dress fabric that was too light in color.

- There was an issue with maintaining dress lengths that were appropriate—not too long or too short. Just below the calf was ideal.

- Young men needed to be more vigilant in wearing their hats whenever outside of the house.

"There will always be style-pushers."

Rose's Priorities

Rose joined the Hummingbirds NWA2 because her brother and cousins were in the group and because she valued its guidelines. The members of the church-based group were committed to staying true to their faith and traditions. There was strong ministerial and parental guidance; all parents and youth met twice each year, and the leaders read the guidelines aloud as a reminder of the expectations. Members could spend time with others in small groups within the larger group at Sunday gatherings but were reminded to avoid Saturday evening events and a "party atmosphere." It was allowable to host a friend or join a sibling and their friend at home on a Saturday evening, but this was not related to dating. Engaging in sports at public parks was to be avoided.

Though it might seem restrictive to some, Rose found her youth group's framework helpful as she moved forward in her faith. She found peace in its familiar embrace and deeply appreciated the friendships she formed.

Subtle variations

There is variation in what is acceptable within youth groups as determined by church and parental leadership. A current trend that started with the youth has women dropping the hem length of their dresses nearly to their ankles. Like teens everywhere, young women may seek to show both their individuality and their solidarity with their group. Maybe the dress fabric (always a solid color) has a subtle texture or embossing, or they may sew a bit of decorative edging on a sleeve. Perhaps a buddy group wears black leggings under their dresses, or enhances the gathers at their dress sleeves, or enlarges the tucks at the shoulder of their capes, or wears athletic socks and sport slides—or cowboy boots—on their feet. Girls in more conservative groups, however, may keep the length of their dresses consistent with what their mothers and grandmothers wear, made in a solid fabric with a smooth finish.

Boys have fewer options to express their individuality through clothes, but some groups may call for their boys to have precise four-corner haircuts rather than bowl cuts or to wear the traditional broadcloth shirt for casual wear instead of a knit polo shirt. Buggies, too, may vary depending on the group's preferences.

"Undercut buggies are great; they can really whip around on a tight radius. A sulky is even more fun!"

The traditional closed carriage is handy when transporting more than two people, but if the weather is nice and the driver is giving another person a ride, they'll look to an open buggy. The style of single-seat, two-person open buggy varies, from a traditional four-wheeled version to a four-wheeled undercut that turns on a dime to the two-wheeled racing-style sulky.

A young man may choose from among a variety of open buggy styles for transportation and courting when the weather is temperate. This undercut four-wheeled model has a small cargo area at the back. JOHN HERR

A newer-style buggy may seem a harmless indulgence to some parents but a step too far to others. There is always safety to consider. Overcrowding is a concern if young people hang out of doors and windows. In a closed carriage, riders are less vulnerable. One grandmother recalls that she and her beau switched to a closed model when they dated fifty years ago because miscreants in cars shouted and threw things at them as they traveled. She worries about her grandchildren when they're out and around.

Getting from here to there

Since youth group members may come from all over Lancaster County—and sometimes as far away as Dauphin, Franklin, York, Chester, or Perry Counties—some travel a considerable distance for a Sunday get-together. It could be well over thirty miles from a member's home to the host's home. Friends who live close together might hire a driver with a car or a van. A large group traveling further might charter a bus or two for the trip.

When traveling twenty or more miles by horse and carriage, a young man can be creative. He might:

- Hitch two horses to his buggy to share the load.
- Stop midway on the drive and visit friends or family while giving his horse a rest.
- Stop at a relative's home and borrow a horse, leaving his horse there and picking it up on the way back.
- Take a multi-leg trip, picking up friends and switching out horses along the way.

If a young man is dating, he may keep a horse at his girlfriend's house. He will drive to her place and leave his original horse there, switch to his secondary horse, and continue to the get-together with his girlfriend. Then he will reverse it on the way home.

To avoid extensive travel in one day, some of the youth may travel to their destination area on Saturday. They will be hosted overnight by friends or relatives who live near where the youth will be meeting. After attending a friend's church service on Sunday morning, they'll participate in the youth group's social time and singing in the afternoon and evening. Then they'll head home late Sunday night.

Our buddies

Young people within each youth group are grouped according to their ages. Girls who join within roughly the same year are designated as "buddy girls," a cluster of eight to twelve young women who are sixteen and seventeen. The young men of a corresponding age are called "buddy guys." Together, the same-age young people are called a "buddy bunch" or "buddy group." They maintain an almost familial relationship, with girls making snack foods and boys supplying the group-owned volleyball net and, often, transportation. The buddies navigate their years in youth group together. In addition to the youngest group, there are usually four or five older buddy groups. Age groupings vary depending on the makeup of the larger group, often with a buddy group for each year or two of age.

Buddy groups within a youth group show solidarity by adopting their own names; for example there are Seahawks, Anchors, and Hurricanes within the Eagles youth group and Tailgaters, Trailblazers, Tornados, Tomahawks, and Torpedoes within the Icebergs.

Though the formation seems somewhat happenstance, buddy group friendships are tremendously important. After learning to know one another as teens, buddy girls—and buddy guys—support one another through their youth group years and beyond. They may date and marry from within their buddy bunch. One young woman loved the idea that maybe her brother would date one of her buddies; then her buddy girl might become her sister-in-law!

When a buddy girl marries, her buddies are invited to wear dresses made of the same fabric as the bride or a complementary color, all matching.

Buddies frequently remain close friends, meeting regularly for visits and trips through the years. They identify themselves by their youth group names from many years earlier.

- Ruthie and Abner married over twenty years ago and socialize regularly with the eleven other couples in their buddy group that formed twenty-five years ago. Occasionally that takes them out of state to visit one of the five other couples, who moved to Amish settlements in Wisconsin, Indiana, and Kentucky.

- Elizabeth and Sylvan, now both seventy-one, recently celebrated their fiftieth wedding anniversary with other couples who married the same year they did. The eleven couples traveled by bus from Lancaster County to Pittsburgh for the weekend and reveled in sightseeing and visiting along the way.

- Sadie, who is eighty-two, still sees her buddy group regularly, though two different-aged buddy groups have joined together. They've all been friends since they were sixteen.

Amish women are generally around twenty-one or twenty-two when they marry, and men a year or two older.[5] But not everyone follows that norm. Youth who reach their mid-twenties and older remain in the oldest buddy group within their youth group. Many of their buddies have married younger and thus left the youth group. As time goes on and more of their contemporaries marry, a cohort of those who are older might form.

Depending on the number of older participants in one's youth group, members in their later twenties and early thirties might move to a youth group with a larger number their age. One offshoot of the Hummingbirds comprises just older young adults. Members of a few groups, called "friend groups," are in their forties and fifties. They value the camaraderie and social activities more than the possibility of romance.

Sunday "singing" schedule

Youth groups meet every Sunday at one of the member's homes from mid-afternoon through late evening. There may be occasions when members visit other groups where their coworkers, cousins, or friends are members. Each meeting follows a specific schedule that includes games, a meal, singing, and snacks. Young women and young men mix to play games; otherwise, the genders socialize separately.

Each member's family hosts a gathering about twice a year. Parents make sure the property is ready for eighty or more guests by preparing an area for volleyball nets in a field or on the lawn, organizing enough tables and benches to accommodate everyone for the meals and singing, and planning and preparing the food. Additional adults such as relatives of the hosts and parents of other youth are welcome to attend; they generally enjoy visiting with each other on the periphery of the action.

When people arrive, between three and four in the afternoon, some jump right into spirited games of volleyball. Others play spikeball or other games or simply socialize. Since volleyball is routinely played during vocational school recesses across the county, nearly everyone has some level of proficiency. If there is inclement weather, space is set up in the barn for volleyball or in the family's recreation room for matches that require less space, like table tennis, spikeball, board games, Memory, and euchre.

Supper is at five o'clock. The host parents may prepare chicken barbecue on the grill and macaroni and cheese; other parents bring salads.

Young men sit at one group of tables or in a certain picnic area, young women at another.

Young women or host parents supply desserts for supper and snacks for later. One of the young women maintains a list with the food needed, then fills in names of who is bringing what. It might be a chocolate trifle or some kind of "delight" (graham cracker crust, cream cheese mixed with whipped cream in the middle, preserved or fresh fruit on top). One group is so fond of whoopie pies that they are not included as a general dessert but appear in a category of their own. This ensures that there will *always* be whoopie pies. Along with the traditional chocolate or pumpkin, there might be chocolate chip or shoofly whoopie pies.

> "Whoopie pies are in a category by themselves."

After supper, there's another hour or so of games, then the singing.

The original "supervised" schedule calls for singing in German from the *Ausbund* from seven to eight, then from the *Gesangbuch* from eight to nine.[6] Some of the groups have adjusted the schedule by shortening the time of singing from each book.

Each youth host and their best friend sits at one end of a long table; a brother or sister (if part of the youth group) and their best friend sit at the other end. The hosts' buddy groups sit on the first bench at the table, girls on one side, boys on the other side. Rows of benches extend back on both sides to seat the remainder of the youth; the group of girls faces the group of boys across the table.

Sunday with the Eagles

Daniel and Rachel were glad to take their turn hosting the Eagles youth group on a spring Sunday. Their two teen daughters, members of the Eagles, had helped clean the recreation room above the horse barn and prepare the food. Now buggies were parked along the driveway and on the lawn, and horses were corralled in the barn. Nearly one hundred youth ages sixteen to their mid-twenties enjoyed the late afternoon sun as they played games or simply visited among themselves. There were

Copies of the Ausbund *and* Gesangbuch *are stacked ready for a Sunday evening singing. Boys sit on the left side; girls sit on the right. The host youth sit at each end of the table with their friends. Buddies of the hosts are seated on benches at the table, with the rest of the youth behind them on benches. Benches for a singing are usually borrowed from the church district; however, these hosts entertain often and have their own set of sturdy plastic benches.* BETH OBERHOLTZER

two volleyball games going on, a pickleball contest, five or six spikeball matches, and a basketball shooting competition.

Other parents, welcome to attend, helped with food and organization. After supper, as seven thirty approached, the dads set up tables and benches for the evening singing. Practiced and welcoming hosts, Daniel and Rachel own dozens of benches to use when entertaining rather than needing to borrow benches from their church district. Though boys and girls mix to play games, they sit separately to sing. Before sitting down, each of the young people lined up to shake hands with the dozens of attending parents, married siblings of the host girls, and friends of the family. Then they took their places to sing. It was beautifully cooperative, with young people taking turns choosing hymns and blending their voices in song. One line from a hymn rang out with special meaning: "When we all get to heaven, what a day of rejoicing that will be!"

The *Ausbund*

Use of the Amish hymnal, the *Ausbund*, connects the present-day
Amish worshiper to previous generations and to their early Anabaptist
forebears. The core hymns were written nearly five hundred years ago by
Anabaptist believers imprisoned in Bavaria; many were later martyred
for their faith.

The German-language hymns in the *Ausbund* consist of words
only; they are essentially poems that are independently matched to a
selection of secular music of the day and sung by memory. The singing
is slow and in unison, without instrumental accompaniment. The hymn
subjects remind worshipers that suffering is to be expected and to stand
firm against the wickedness of the world. But there is assurance that God
will not forsake his people. Page 770 (song number 131, or "Das Loblied")
is sung at the beginning of every Amish worship service: "O Gott Vater,
wir loben Dich und deine Güte preisen" ("O God, Father, we praise you
and your kindness we praise").

The *Ausbund* is understood to be the oldest hymnbook in continu-
ous use in any Christian church anywhere in the world.

The singing is begun by the host, boy or girl. The first song is always
page 770 in the *Ausbund*—"Das Loblied"—often followed by the song on
page 738. The German words can be matched with a variety of tunes.
Depending on the youth group's traditions, singing may be in unison or in
parts. Four verses may be sung in one tune, then the next four verses in
another tune—the first forty-four verses carrying perhaps ten different
tunes. Then a jump to a verse later in the hymn (the page 738 hymn has
seventy-one verses) and still more tunes.

After singing from the *Ausbund*, the group sings from the *Gesangbuch*,
also in German but often in four-part harmony. There is still a mix-and-
match aspect to the lyrics and tunes. One youth group might occasionally
translate from English to German so the words fit the gospel tune.
Another group might sing the verses of each song in German, then the

 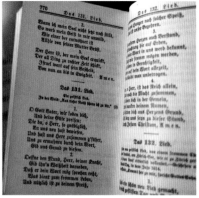

Regular gatherings of large groups at homes—youth group events, church services, and weddings—are supported by the contents of the bench wagon. The wagon brings benches for seating and copies of the Ausbund *and* Gesangbuch *for the singing. "Das Loblied" (Song of Praise) on page 770 of the* Ausbund *is always the first or second hymn sung at the weekly youth gatherings.* **LEFT:** JOHN HERR, **RIGHT:** CHRISTY KAUFFMAN

choruses in English. Each group maintains what is important while fine-tuning the details.

Since singing in church is in unison, young people often learn to sing in four-part harmony at "note classes" or "singing classes" that are held for eight-week periods. And if the host who leads out singing has difficulty? Rose, of the Hummingbirds NWA2, explained, "If they start at the wrong pitch, everyone will begin there but correct it as they go along. And if they again start on the wrong pitch, everybody else will be ready to fix it."

After the singing, young people socialize and snack—host parents supply chips and drinks, and the young women provide a variety of fiber balls and dessert bars. Those interested in further socializing before heading home might gather again to sing, this time perhaps gospel songs in English.

Other times to socialize

In addition to the weekly meetups, there are other times to connect: trips to sing to the elderly, picnics, swimming, cookouts, ice-skating, and holiday get-togethers. Buddy girls or buddy guys might go on trips (not together) to the Jersey Shore or to a cabin in the woods. There are opportunities close to home or trips out of state to serve others together: cooking for a fundraiser, cleaning up after a fire, rebuilding after a disaster.

Religious days like Easter Monday, Pentecost, Ascension Day, and Second Christmas are Amish holidays that call for time off from work. For many Amish young people, that means a day of socializing, games, and a meal together—with recognition of the day's meaning. There may be baseball or volleyball tournaments. Gatherings also take place on secular holidays; on Thanksgiving, the sport may be touch football.

Each bench wagon transports about forty benches of varying lengths as well as twenty chairs—plus boxes of hymnals. BETH OBERHOLTZER

Some youth groups hold baseball tournaments at public parks on religious holidays. Others play baseball or volleyball on members' private fields. BETH OBERHOLTZER

THREE

Courtship and Engagement

Traveling to and from youth gatherings gives a couple time to get to know each other. DOUG HOOVER

Dating is not a frivolous endeavor for Amish youth. It is always done with the goal of finding a life partner. A girl might have noticed a special guy, but she does not make the first move or engage with him beyond general friendliness. Flirting to compete for attention is rare. "We don't want to exalt one over another. It's important to keep everyone on the same level," said one young woman.

Dating

Though young people sometimes meet their potential life partners in youth group, that is not the sole reason to socialize. As one mom said, "They can't have fun if that's the only thing!" A couple may initially meet outside of youth group—perhaps when attending a wedding, while volunteering together with a disaster relief organization, or through friends or cousins. When they begin dating, they visit each other's youth groups. After a few weeks the boy will join the girl's youth group, and they will regularly attend together.

Amish youth show a striking willingness to submit to what they understand to be God's plan for their lives. A girl waits for a boy to ask her out with the certainty that the boy has prayerfully considered it.

Her parents may know his family and offer their opinion; his parents might offer him guidance. It is not required, but some young men ask the young woman's father for permission to take her out.

An outsider may find it hard to understand that girls are comfortable waiting to be asked out rather than indicating an interest themselves. But that doesn't mean it's easy for the boys. One aunt recalls that her nephew asked out multiple girls, who all refused him. He persevered, and as Aunt Elizabeth said, "He got the best of the bunch."

Benjy and Marian

Benjy caught Marian's eye when she first joined the Eagles youth group at sixteen. He was just seventeen, and they were both too young to think about dating. She briefly went out with someone else when she was eighteen but broke it off—perhaps with Benjy in mind. Marian privately hoped he would make a move, but if he wasn't available when she was, she would accept it. "If the timing is off, it isn't meant to be," she said.

Three or four months later, Benjy asked Marian out. They dated for two years, then married when they were twenty and twenty-one.

In some of the more conservative communities, a couple's first several dates consist of the young man taking the young woman home on Sunday evening after the singing and visiting with her at her home. The couple might not tell anyone except their best friends that they are going out. The two simply leave the Sunday gathering, quietly, at the same time, and he takes her home. Others may not even notice that they left together, but when they realize, it causes a stir. "Did you see Aaron took Annie home?" people may exclaim. After a few weeks, he picks her up at her home and takes her to the singing and home afterward.

In other communities, a first date involves the young man picking the young woman up at her home, talking with her parents, taking her to youth group, then returning her home afterward. Friends occasionally make a big fuss about the couple's first date. They may decorate the guy's buggy with balloons or streamers and write "Congratulations!" on the windows. One buggy sported a sign on the back suggesting, "Honk your horn! First date!"

Andrew and Emma

When Andrew took Emma home from youth group on their first date one Sunday evening, their fellow *yunges* (young people) lined the farm lane and clapped and cheered as they drove out. The outside of the carriage was dotted with messages on sticky notes such as "Wishing you the best in this new step." Inside on the seat was a bottle of sparkling cider and two goblets. Strings of tiny battery-powered lights hung from the ceiling. Emma's buddy girls had crept out after supper and before the singing to decorate.

Andrew confessed to his brother that his heart was pounding because of all the attention. His older sister, not overly sympathetic, thought a little discomfort would do him good. "It will make a man out of him," she said. "It will help him mature."

If it's not too late when the couple arrives back at the girl's home, her parents will greet them, then leave the pair to enjoy time together and have a snack. If the boy has a several-hours-long drive ahead of him and work in the morning, the visit will be short. He may have a bit of a nap on the way since his horse generally knows its way on the home stretch.

Ivan and Naomi

Naomi was twenty and had known Ivan, twenty-five, for the three years that they were in youth group together, but she'd never thought of dating him—until he left a message for her on her family's answering machine. "I want to talk to you," he said. "I'll call you on Thursday evening at seven thirty."

She immediately knew he was calling to ask her to date him. It was unexpected and a little disconcerting,

"That was God, definitely."

but her parents knew his family and respected them. She considered the idea and prayed about it. Ultimately, Naomi realized she didn't really have a reason to say no and was open to the idea of getting to know Ivan. So she agreed when he asked whether he could take her to youth group and home again. Ivan planned the timing so he could drive his horse from his home in Strasburg to hers in Kinzers, then just a short distance farther to the youth gathering that week.

Ivan continued to pick Naomi up and take her home from youth group each week, even when the distance was much further. Naomi enjoyed spending time with him and knew dating him was a good decision. When Ivan proposed a few years later, Naomi had every reason to say yes!

If the couple does not belong to the same youth group, when they start dating the young man will begin attending the young woman's group. If they live more than fifteen or so miles apart, after a few dates he may leave a horse at her place so he has a fresh horse to drive to youth group meetings. Jay was so sure of his and Rose's compatibility that he had one of his horses trucked to her house before they even had their first date!

To avoid traveling long distances several times in one weekend, a dating couple often spends the weekend at his or her home. They spend Saturday evenings visiting, eating, and relaxing with family or with married siblings. If friends of the couple visit at one of their homes, the friends routinely spend the night; households are accustomed to hosting groups.

When the couple is engaged or clearly committed to each other, they plan visits to aunts and uncles and grandparents to learn to know each other's extended families. If church meets that Sunday, the couple usually goes with the family. Though they don't sit together (men and women sit separately), they arrive and leave together.

The two rarely see each other on weekdays unless there's a significant family event to celebrate. If the couple is dating seriously, their social circle expands to include married buddies. This is a move toward cementing their identity as a twosome.

Dating is commonly understood to be a precursor to marriage. If one of a committed dating couple passes away, the remaining partner is involved in planning the funeral service and is included in the deceased partner's family events going forward.

Gideon and Leah

At age fifteen, Leah was quite shy. She kind of liked the looks of the young man who came to lay linoleum at her family's home, but she only talked with him briefly.

A few years later, Leah's sister's youth group met at their home. Leah decided to stay home rather than go to her own youth group gathering. It was winter, so the youth played games in the barn instead of volleyball outside. *Yunges* were all over the place playing table tennis, shuffleboard, spikeball, and the card game Rook.

Vernon washes his courting buggy on Saturday, getting it ready for Sunday when he will pick up Lydia Ann to take her to their youth group gathering. BETH OBERHOLTZER

Gideon, the linoleum guy and a member of Leah's sister's youth group, immediately recognized Leah and invited her to play table tennis. She didn't quite remember him, but he very clearly had thought of her. When asked about it nearly twenty years later, he deadpanned, "It was a fun game." Gideon and Leah have been married fourteen years and have five children. They live in the farmhouse where Leah grew up, walking across that linoleum every day for years. And they have a Ping-Pong table.

It is not unusual for a young woman to end up marrying the first guy she dates, nor is it unusual for her to have dated one or two—or even three—guys previously. If it doesn't work out, couples generally make a mutual decision to break up. It could be as simple as John, twenty-one, described: "It's not going anywhere, so why go on?" If a young man has his eye on a girl who dated someone previously, he'll wait three or four months to ask her out himself. If someone else beats him to it and she accepts the other guy? It's understood that it must not have been right for them.

If a couple has dated for more than six months, they are likely in it for the long haul. They will continue dating for another year or two, depending on their ages, and then start planning a wedding.

There is a general expectation that young people will begin dating in their early twenties or younger and marry when they're in their early or mid-twenties. But dating and marriage don't always happen on the expected timeline.

Annie Is Independent

At age twenty-six, Annie lived at home with her parents and six younger siblings. Though she was active in a youth group and had close friends there, she was not dating anyone. She said, "Sixteen is way too young to date. If you date then, do you marry at eighteen? I don't think a girl should be tied down; the best time of running around is ages sixteen, seventeen, eighteen . . . I wouldn't have wanted to start dating then. One girlfriend of mine was single until she started dating at twenty-five. She missed doing whatever she wanted whenever she wanted since her boyfriend expected to spend weekends with her. It was a hard adjustment at first. Now she enjoys spending time with him. They visit and get to know each other's families on Saturday evenings and go to Sunday evening youth group gatherings together.

"My friends who got married at nineteen look at me and wish they could travel the way I do. They ask where I get all this money. Well, they're home with a husband and a couple of children and don't have their own money—or the time to run around.

"People sometimes ask me when I'm going to get married. Why do I have to get married?"

Most youth groups include members from age sixteen into their mid-twenties. Since members leave the group when they marry, there are fewer members in the older age brackets. Young people heading toward their thirties and older may leave a youth-centric group to join a group that has generally older members.

One mother was not at all concerned that her son didn't start dating his future wife until he was in his early thirties. He married her when he was in his mid-thirties. "He had four unmarried friends the same age, and they had a good time running around," she said. However, one wedding season found them all marrying, and their brides were in their late twenties and early thirties.

Steven and Priscilla

Priscilla felt like it was time for a change. She was twenty-two and her younger sister was engaged; close friends in her youth group were leaving to get married. She'd dated a bit, but it didn't really click with the guy.

The new group she joined was a better fit; most members were older, and it included other girls who were teachers. They had great fun at their weekly get-togethers. She took no notice of Steven. Even when her mom asked what she thought of him, Priscilla just responded, "Oh, Mom. He's

Couples easily sit side by side in buggies when courting and may squash together when traveling with friends, but public displays of affection are unlikely. DOUG HOOVER

too old." A month later, Steven, thirty-three, surprised her by asking her to date him.

Priscilla gave it two weeks of serious thought. She spoke with her parents and prayed about it. There was the ten-year age difference to consider, but he was a kind man from a good family and not too hard on the eyes. She said yes to going out with him. Within a few weeks, she was telling her mom, "I don't know exactly why, but it just feels okay." Then in a few months it was, "Dad, for some reason, I just love him."

They married a little over a year after their first date. Steven has taken over his home farm, where Priscilla helps out and tends their three young children.

Amish couples meet the old-fashioned way: in person. They don't need to worry about cultural clashes or differing religions. There is a wide network of friends and relatives who can vouch for the potential date's character based on knowing them or their extended family. This allows a young person to focus on the personality and innate qualities of their possible partner while knowing that they likely agree on the important things. They both have the same expectation of roles in a marriage.

Abram and Susan

Abram and Susan grew up just three miles apart and were friends since they were sixteen and joined the same youth group. They saw each other at gatherings each week. When they got older, each dated someone else. Over the years, couples in their intersecting circles of friends paired off and began dating—some going on to marry.

One spring evening, over seven years after Abram and Susan first met, Susan's family was at the supper table talking about that day's baseball tournament when they heard a knock on the door. Susan's dad opened the door. "Hey, Abe! What can I do for you?" Their voices got quiet. Everyone strained to hear. Abram was asking if he could talk to Susan. The two took a walk and talked about lots of things. Abram first asked if they could share a friendship, then asked whether she would be willing to date him. Susan said she would call him with her answer after she got home from work the next day.

She explained, "I didn't get much sleep that night. In the morning I knew what I was going to say, but I didn't know if it would be the same in the evening."

Abram spent an anxious day at work building decks. What would she say? She called him at nine that evening; her answer was, "Yes, I'll date you." They got married a year later.

Engagement

Observers keep a keen eye on dating couples and enjoy speculating about when the pair might decide to marry. A young couple that begins dating at eighteen or so may date for several years before deciding to get married. A couple that begins dating in their twenties will often decide more quickly: perhaps dating for less than a year before a spring engagement is followed by a fall wedding. Upon engagement, there is no diamond ring or dramatic announcement. Though the couple is clearly happy to be together, they don't advertise it far and wide—but they don't keep it a secret either.

In past generations, the announcement of the wedding date was made in as little as a few weeks or a month before the wedding. Even though a couple had likely picked a date well ahead of time, they were quiet about it. Humility kept them from bringing attention to themselves and the event.

Family and friends might have looked for clues about whether a wedding was planned. A long row of celery planted in the garden might be for creamed celery at the wedding dinner. Sometimes, in the spirit of mischief, the couple got a kick out of misleading people.

A newer interpretation of humility allows that acknowledgment of the upcoming wedding does not automatically become prideful and that it is perfectly acceptable to share the couple's joy ahead of time.

Another piece of the new transparency regarding upcoming weddings concerns travel plans. With a growing population and family and friends in other states who need to arrange transportation, the bride's family may send out "save the date" postcards or notify people by phone. The family needs to make reservations well ahead for items such as a wedding house, kitchen appliances, wedding trailers, dish chests, and bench wagons. Actual invitations are mailed roughly a month ahead. They may be simple handwritten notes or professionally printed cards. The bride and groom personally visit friends and family to ask them to tend them at the Eck (the corner of the table where they sit at the wedding meals) or act as side sitters (attendants).

It is not necessary for a would-be groom to ask permission of the bride's father to marry her, but it is done on occasion. Since the family has hosted the boyfriend innumerable times, it would not be a surprise that a proposal was imminent.

There are essentially two phases to a couple's engagement: prior to publication (the formal church announcement) and after publication. Different behavior is customary in these two periods.

Prior to publication

Upon telling others of their engagement, a couple continues attending their usual youth group functions. However, they may arrive at a Sunday gathering late, maybe just in time for supper, rather than an hour or two earlier to participate in games. Friends may start to tease them, saying, "Do you have plans for this fall?" If it is the norm for the young men in their youth group not to wear hats (except to church), an engaged man may begin wearing a hat like the married men do.

In addition to enjoying meals with each other's families and married siblings, they also socialize with other dating and engaged couples.

A typical engagement gift from a young man to his intended might be a clock, a dozen settings of china, or a water set (pitcher and glasses). Sometimes a young engaged woman is celebrated at a home shopping party attended by twenty or thirty young women friends and relatives. Along with games and snacks, the guests can purchase items from the bride's wish list. Or there may simply be a small, girls-only gathering to celebrate the bride.

An upcoming wedding might prompt a young person who was previously baptized to reexamine their commitment to Christ and the church and, if they have violated their vows, to make confession to church leadership. Examples of violations may include driving a car, drinking alcohol,

One young man delighted his intended bride with an engagement gift of a water set that included a pitcher and six goblets. CHRISTY KAUFFMAN

or using drugs. Sexual immorality is much less common, but it is a more serious offense. Depending on the severity of the infraction, the steps to bring them back to the church likely include a six-week (or more) excommunication, during which there is a series of meetings with the ministers, then congregational assent, for readmittance. It is a proving time in which a member's sincerity and cooperation will help them regain lost trust. And it is a warning from the church that there are consequences for sin.

Some young people may delay joining the church until a few months before they get married; then they can avoid having to make confession. But one mom expressed concern they might be "giving themselves into the hands of the devil" if they postpone.

If a couple confesses to the sin of sexual intercourse before marriage, the wedding will take place as soon as possible and the guest list is scaled back. The bride is not allowed to wear a white cape and apron, and the festivities are shortened. Instead of a daylong celebration, guests leave right after supper. If a woman marries a man who confessed to previous sexual relations, but she has not, she wears a white cape and apron to marry.

This kind of confession is rarely made. Susie, seventy-four, has only been a part of two or three church services over the years when the sin of sexual impurity was confessed by individuals before their wedding.

Church communities take privacy very seriously; they don't talk to outsiders about sensitive issues that come up. Annie's friend made a confession at his church, but she has no idea why, and she won't ask him. "Pretty much what goes on in your church stays in your church," she said.

Though parental consent to marry is not required, the engaged couple must receive several other important permissions to marry within the Amish church. Before anything else, they must have been baptized into the church and be members in good standing—or "in order." If the young woman or young man had been pushing the boundaries of church-sanctioned behavior, they have now stepped back into line. The process of gaining permissions begins right after October 11, which is Fast Day (a day in which church members fast from midnight until noon, reading the scriptures and prayer books, thoughtfully preparing for the upcoming

Young couples are fortunate to have older relatives who model the kind of marriage they may wish for themselves. Daadi *and* Mammi *(Grandpa and Grandma) are ready and willing to encourage and advise. The different generations enjoy one another's company and keep one another up to date about who's doing what.* JOHN HERR

communion church services). Publication in church of the upcoming wedding generally occurs a few weeks or a month after Fast Day.

A young man seeking to be married pays a visit to the deacon in his home church. The deacon is likely to be someone whose family has known his own family for years and with whom the groom-to-be has a good relationship. But this is not a casual conversation. First, the young man explains that he is hoping to be married and gives the name of his intended, confirming that she wishes to marry him. He then requests a letter signed by the bishop and other church ministers that attests he is a member in good standing. He needs to confirm that if he was previously behaving outside of the *Ordnung*, it is no longer the case. In response to a direct question, he affirms that he is free from fornication. (It is a pro forma question, just as it is when the bride is asked the same thing by her deacon. If there was an issue, it would have been dealt with previously.)

If all is in order, the groom-to-be picks up the testimonial letter (called *Zeignis*) after it is signed and pays a visit to the deacon in his intended bride's church district. He introduces himself and hands over the letter. The *Zeignis* confirms that the brother is in good standing ("in peace") and requests prayer. It is signed by all ministers of his district. The groom-to-be's deacon acts as a go-between and visits the bride-to-be briefly—perhaps with her mother or parents present—who confirms her desire to marry her suitor. She is also questioned about whether she is "in order" with the church *Ordnung* and whether she has "remained pure," questions that she can easily answer in the affirmative. If the bride and groom are members of the same church, that church's deacon first confirms that the young man is in good standing, then visits the young woman.

Since the young woman would have recently taken communion in her church, the church ministers know she is in good standing, so a separate *Zeignis* is not needed to confirm it.

When the blessing of the church is given, everything is set for the wedding to go forward.

Publication and after

Communion in the Amish church is held twice a year: in the spring and in the fall. Fall communion takes place the Sunday after Fast Day. At the end of the service on the next church Sunday, the bride's deacon announces any weddings in the district that are coming up in the fall. Given that the district may include multiple young people of marriageable age, several upcoming weddings may be published at the same time. After the deacon's announcement, the father of the bride gives the wedding date and invites all adult members of the congregation to attend. Depending on the number of guests that can be accommodated, the cutoff may be age sixteen, eighteen, or twenty and older. Moses, the father of eight girls who are now grown, was adamant that it was important to invite as many as possible to his daughters' weddings. Church members are the first to show up when there's a fire, a medical crisis, or a death. Moses wanted church people to be there to celebrate the good times too.

Since wedding season has expanded into the spring, additional weddings are now published in the late winter or early spring.

The couple does not attend church on publication day. The bride makes a special lunch for her intended and they enjoy a brief period of being alone before the whirl of wedding preparation engulfs them. When her parents and siblings arrive home from church in the afternoon, they welcome her young man into the family. The bride's mother makes a celebratory evening supper for the whole family.

The couple makes their final appearance at their youth group gathering on the Sunday evening, between supper and the singing, on the day their engagement is published. Though they've been engaged—and friends aware of it—for months, this is a time to celebrate. The couple hands out wedding invitations to their friends and receives congratulations. The entire youth group of eighty to one hundred is often invited to attend the festivities, perhaps excepting the youngest buddy group. There's good-natured ribbing in the form of the repeated question, "Are we invited? Are we invited?"

The soon-to-be-married couple is undergoing a major transition. They are committed to moving forward together while their individual support systems are also evolving based on their partnership status. They segue

When away from home, Amish children and adults cover their heads. Women and girls wear coverings and men and boys wear hats. A man's hat style and brim size is related to his age and marital status. JOHN HERR

from participation in buddy groups of single friends to visiting with other dating couples to mixing primarily with engaged or newly married couples. The couple need not experience the journey alone.

Even something as distinct to a couple as going to the county courthouse to get their marriage license becomes a social event as multiple engaged couples split the cost of renting a van and head for Lancaster City.

After publication and before their wedding, the couple does not attend church services. They spend weekends together and visit with family and other couples.

Traditionally, the groom-to-be moves in with the bride's family several weeks before the wedding to help prepare. (Though it might sound scandalous, it is not. The groom has already spent many weekends at the bride's home while courting, and now, as then, he sleeps in a separate bedroom.) The exact timing of the move depends on how soon the wedding will take place after the publication date, how much work is yet to be done, and the details of transportation to his job. If the bride's family farms, the groom's help is vital for cleaning up the property and preparing the building and grounds.

The joining of a couple in marriage is clearly the joining of two families.

Remaining single

Though virtually the whole of Amish culture is built around marrying and raising a family, there are those—certainly a minority—who live perfectly satisfying lives without having married.

When young women reach their late twenties and early thirties and young men their early thirties, it may be awkward for them to remain in a youth group when their contemporaries have left the group and gotten married. Sometimes the older "unmarrieds" move into a youth group whose members are largely in their thirties and perhaps up to forty.

If a man has not gotten married by his late thirties—perhaps an invited girl declined to date him, or he and a girlfriend parted ways, or he is simply disinclined to date—he will likely stop attending the youth group and settle in as a single. He may continue to live with his parents, share housing with a sibling or other relative, or live on his own. His job supports him easily, and he is still comfortably part of his family and community.

If a woman has not gotten married by her early thirties, things aren't quite as easy for her. Since an Amish woman's identity is tied closely to her husband and children, the "maiden lady" needs to find meaning outside of that. And since women generally do less work outside the home than men and get paid less, finances can be an issue.

- Tasked with caring for others from a young age, an unmarried woman may take on the persona of caregiver within the extended family. While maintaining an outside job, she may also help in the households of married siblings when new babies come along or when there is illness. She might live at home with her parents and become their caretaker as they age.

- Or she may become somewhat of a career woman who owns a bookshop or a cleaning business or who teaches school, an independent woman who does what she wishes with her time and money. She may live with a sister or friend—or on her own. Family and community remain important.

Esther talked about young women who were edging toward being "old maids" who did not consider it a bad thing at all. She explained that most would have had a chance to date but didn't for some reason. "I have a niece who is planning for her old-maid house," she said.

Leah is thirty-three, married, and just had her fifth child. She has a close friend her age who is not married and lives on her own. "Marie is happy, content, and loves children," said Leah. "She helps with family and works in a fabric store. She's a blessing." Leah described close conversations with her friend Marie. "It was not always like this for her, but she made a decision to choose contentment."

In Amish culture, satisfaction is to be found where one is rather than wishing for something different. Laura, mother of seven and grandmother of five, noted, "If someone can't find spiritual contentment in being single, they won't be content in marriage."

As women and men reach their forties and beyond and remain unmarried, they begin to take on the manner and dress of their married counterparts.

- Instead of sitting with the young people at church, they join their same-age cohort of married men or women.

- Women exchange the white apron of a single woman for the black apron of a married woman.

- Men switch to the style of hat favored by the married men rather than the single men. If a man remains unmarried into his fifties, he will likely grow a beard.

Even if someone has settled happily into the single life, they likely remain open to the possibility of marriage. It is common for men whose wives have passed away to remarry, often to younger women. Women who are widowed might also remarry. Jacob's wife died of cancer, and they had three young children. When he was in his thirties, he reconnected with a woman, also in her thirties, whom he remembered from their common youth group years earlier.

Eli and Betty

Betty was perfectly satisfied with her life as a single woman when she entered her forties. She enjoyed taking care of her birds and dogs and working with her horses. Though she lived with her parents—her brother and his family were on the adjoining farm—she valued her independence. "I was used to coming and going," she said. "I had my horses. I took life as it came. But I didn't say, 'I don't want to marry.' We don't know what God has planned."

Then Eli wrote and said he wanted to come and see her. It was really no surprise. "I guess he thought of me," she said. She allowed Eli to visit, even though she had refused another guy who had tried to woo her by saying he had room for her horses.

Eli's wife had passed away a few years earlier. Betty knew Eli somewhat, and her dad vouched for him. She declined to share courting details,

Betty emphasized that it's important for couples to maintain separate interests. But her husband Eli sometimes lends a hand when she takes care of her Haflinger horses. JOHN HERR

except to say, "Just like young people do . . . after a while we got married." This was when Betty was in her forties and Eli in his sixties. "It's amazing how things happen," Betty said. She took three horses into the marriage. Since Betty hadn't been married before, they had a traditional wedding. The celebration at her brother's farm hosted around four hundred guests and ended shortly after supper instead of going late into the evening.

Twenty years later, the meadow next to Eli and Betty's home has a half dozen or more horses that she dotes on. Eli and Betty don't have children but are very close to their nieces and nephews.

Weddings and marriage are clearly not for everyone. Malinda is a single woman in her late sixties who worked for more than forty years in laundry services. She is now partially retired and lives with her sister. She contended quite firmly that "there's a life without marriage." In fact, she's not very fond of weddings. "I avoid them if I can," she said. "But when I go, I go for the food."

FOUR

Wedding Planning and Preparation

The whole family pitched in to get the bride's home farm ready for the next day's guests.
CHRISTY KAUFFMAN

Samuel's daughter was due to marry in early December. Seeing the work yet to be done around the farm, Samuel remarked that a light, early winter snowfall would make everything look clean and neat. It didn't snow, but a golden sunrise on the morning of the wedding lent a beautiful warm glow to the frost-covered fields.

Wedding location

Amish weddings are held at the home of the bride. Families spend months preparing so the property is in tip-top shape. The upcoming celebration can be viewed as an excellent motivation to finish planned improvements like painting the house or clearing out the barn. Decorative vegetation is pruned and mulched to within an inch of its life. In the spring prior to a fall wedding, great thought is given to landscaping. Do bushes need to be cut back or reshaped? What flowers and greenery should be planted so they're at their best at the right time? How about eucalyptus to decorate the gift area? What other decorative plantings might the bride like? Vegetable gardens may be planted with long rows of potatoes, cabbage, and peppers that will be ready to harvest in the fall.

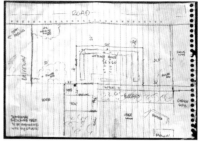

The overhead view the day before Rose's wedding closely matches her carefully drawn plans. **LEFT:** CHRISTY KAUFFMAN, **RIGHT:** BETH OBERHOLTZER

If a bride-to-be is the youngest in the family and she and her parents have moved to a smaller home and turned their farm over to an older brother, her wedding may take place at her brother and sister-in-law's place—the home farm.

In past years, many families kept word of a wedding under wraps until just a few weeks before the date. If members of the community saw an unusual amount of property cleanup and repairs, they couldn't help but speculate. And long rows of covered celery were a dead giveaway since it's nearly impossible to have an Amish wedding without creamed celery on the menu.

David and Fanny live in a large farmhouse that includes in-law quarters, divided from the main house by a set of sliding wooden doors. When they host a church service, those doors—and all other interior doors—are opened to allow the whole first floor of the house to serve as a meeting room. When their daughter got married, the benches filled the room and the porch from wall to wall and had space for four hundred guests. A temporary addition provided space to prepare meals.

When Samuel's daughter got married—as when his family hosts church—he cleared the machinery and wagons out of his implement barn. His wife and daughters, plus the bride-to-be's aunts and girl cousins, scrubbed the walls, windows, and floors to make it ready to house the rows of benches for the service. They created a wedding kitchen in a connected room and rented four stoves to prepare food for the guests.

Samuel's equipment barn (top) has a huge space for the wedding room, another room to serve as the wedding kitchen, a small Eck kitchen, and a recreation room to host singing and gift-opening. Lined up outside are bench wagons, a cooler trailer, and a women's restroom trailer. Omar built a temporary addition to his barn (above) to house the wedding kitchen when his daughter married. A cooler trailer is parked outside. **TOP:** BETH OBERHOLTZER, **BOTTOM:** JOHN HERR

Jacob built a wedding house to abut his farmhouse when his first daughter got married several years ago, then took it down and stored the pieces in his barn. He and a team of helpers reconstructed it for his second daughter's fall wedding. BETH OBERHOLTZER

When the first (and usually oldest) daughter in the family gets married, she paves the way for her sisters. Her parents may have already speculated about where a wedding could take place on their property. But upon an engagement, they get serious with the measuring tape. Already accustomed to hosting several hundred for church services once or twice a year, they look again at their house, barn, and outbuildings with an eye toward hosting up to five hundred.

Many Amish do not have homes or outbuildings large enough to accommodate the expected guests. For them, a temporary addition of some sort is the answer. It may be a large room added along the side of the house, a porch built in, or a structure erected on the driveway.

One Amish entrepreneur saw a need and responded. He and his sons designed and built several wedding houses that are available for rent. Unlike those that consist of labeled pieces that need to be assembled in place, then taken apart after the wedding, these structures remain intact for transport. When compacted, they are roughly the size of a mobile home and are hauled by a tractor. When on-site, the sides slide out to create a room; when fully opened, the largest structure measures thirty-six feet by sixty feet. Four to five hundred wedding guests can be seated when the rows of benches are in place.

After the wedding space has been determined, arrangements must be made for the proper number of benches. Each church district maintains a bench wagon to house and transport the backless benches to homes for hosting church services. Each bench wagon contains fifty to sixty benches of various lengths and a chest with over a hundred hymnals (the *Ausbund* and *Gesangbuch*), along with two dozen or so folding chairs to seat the ministers, bridal party, and older members of the congregation. Depending on the number of anticipated guests, a wedding might require bench wagons from three church districts.

In addition to the wedding room where the church service—and later the meals and singings—are held, adjacent space is assigned to what is essentially a pop-up kitchen. Sinks, stoves, and refrigerators are lined up with plumbing and propane hookup. Eight or more long tables provide work surfaces for the dozen-plus cooks. The wedding kitchen may be set up in the basement, or it may be a temporary addition or in a stand-alone unit. A smaller kitchen area, with its own sink, stove, and cooler, is reserved for the Eck tenders, who prepare special dishes for the bride and groom and display food gifts from guests.

This bride's parents rented a wedding house, portable toilets, and a cooler trailer for their daughter's fall wedding. CHRISTY KAUFFMAN

If needed, a completely equipped cook trailer can be rented. It contains all the appliances, racks and portable shelves, cook pots, place settings, and serving dishes needed to prepare and serve meals for hundreds. The cook trailer can be set up abutting the wedding house. After the wedding room benches are transformed into tables, there is easy passage from the kitchen to what is now the dining room.

A room in the house or the recreation room (which might be in the basement or above the stable or workshop) is set aside to collect and display gifts. In most districts, youth and family gather here immediately after the first dinner seating to sing to the bride and groom while they open gifts.

Additional rooms or areas are made available for cohorts of different ages and genders to gather before the service. Typically, married women gather in the wedding room and married men in the barn; youth girls collect in a bedroom or other room in the house, and youth boys in a section of the barn or other outbuilding; mothers have a space to tend fussy or napping babies, perhaps in the home's living room.

The bride's father is usually called upon to draw out a plan of the property showing where things are to be set up. The plan confirms that all fits where anticipated, then serves as a reference for volunteers and vendors.

Rose's family reserved a wedding house that was set up in the front yard. There was a covered walkway leading into the basement wedding kitchen and into the Eck kitchen and display area. Careful notes on Rose's site map indicated flower beds, driveways, the site for gifts, location of temporary structures, and parking for buggies.

Many guests travel by horse and carriage to attend a wedding. After the horses are unhitched, they are housed in the barn or in a meadow. The family rents horse feeders appropriate to the space available and the number of horses expected. If necessary, a rented tent shades the horses in sunny weather and, with the sides down, keeps them warm in cold weather.

In the week before the wedding, multiple portable toilets are hauled in and placed strategically. On the wedding day, great care is taken to make sure the toilets remain clean and well supplied. Helpers are assigned the jobs of sanitizing them regularly and replenishing soap and paper goods as needed at the wash stations.

The bride and her family

An Amish mother is naturally delighted at her daughter's happiness upon engagement. But she also can't help looking ahead to the massive organizational task awaiting her. Household planning and maintenance take on a new significance. The common phrasing among the Amish—that a family is "making" a wedding—hints at the skill and creativity required.

Women aren't suddenly thrown into the task of organizing meals and events for hundreds—they're eased into it. Girls routinely help cook for their families when they're growing up. Upon marriage they make meals for their own families, which may expand to include six or more children. Hosting church twice a year means organizing the food for more than two hundred people, and parents host youth groups of eighty or more when their children are in their teens and twenties.

A woman in her forties has likely attended over two hundred weddings thus far. Chances are she has performed a variety of tasks at family weddings and has a good idea of how her daughter's wedding day should unfold. Older sisters and friends pass along lists and tips. There are several published wedding planners available that focus on the needs of the Amish in Lancaster County. Relatives stand ready to help.

For an Amish mother, putting together a wedding for her first daughter is the biggest challenge. There are perhaps several more daughters coming along, so she keeps reams of notes for subsequent weddings as she works her way through this one. Lists and plans are all handwritten. Though there is a pattern to the day, daughters have different personalities and preferences to consider.

Lydia's first daughter got married last year, and they're making a wedding for her second daughter this year. As exciting as this all is, Lydia is somewhat relieved that her third daughter, twenty-one-year-old Sylvia, isn't dating anyone right now. But that could change quickly.

Who is invited to the wedding?

When weddings are held in the bride's home, the maximum number of guests who can be squeezed into the house might top out at 350 to 400. A wedding held in a barn or outbuilding or wedding house can accommodate many more. It's not unusual for a modern guest list to exceed 500. The Amish are known for their large families, so the numbers climb quickly. Moses and Susie have fourteen grown children, nearly one hundred grandchildren, and thirty great-grandchildren. In addition to family, there are the long-time friends of the bride's parents, the bride's and groom's buddy groups, other youth group friends, coworkers, and people from the bride's church.

Most Amish weddings host some English guests; they may include close neighbors, non-Amish family members, and coworkers.

Upon an engagement, a wedding date is chosen, and word of it spreads quickly. Family and friends at a distance are notified by mail or phone. Church people from the bride's district are invited by the bride's father at the end of a service. The groom's friends and relatives are invited, but not the members of his church district beyond that. The engaged couple and the bride's parents personally invite those who perform tasks for the wedding; other guests receive mailed invitations.

Schoolchildren are thrilled to be invited if their teacher is the bride; some of the older boys might be tapped to serve as hostlers (those who care for the horses and do barn chores). Invitations often reference the holy nature of the joining and include the words "Lord willing" or "If it is in His will."

The couple chooses their side sitters, an important role, months ahead of the wedding date. Each partner selects an unmarried boy and girl—siblings, cousins, or close friends—who are paired for the day. The two girls are attendants to the bride, and the two boys accompany the groom. The couple also invites three or four married couples—from among siblings, close friends, and relatives—to act as their personal waitstaff for the day. The couples are called "Eck tenders" because they tend the bridal pair who sit at the Eck (corner) of the wedding dinner table.

Dressing the bride and attendants

On their wedding day, Amish brides wear a solid-colored dress, a white (or black) head covering, a white cape and apron, black stockings, and black high-top shoes.

Young women, even within the specific guidelines, manage to introduce bits of individuality. Wedding dress colors have customarily been a dark to medium shade of blue or purple. More recently, fabric is chosen from a broader color palette—including charcoal, gray, and dark wine. Dark green has also risen in popularity. After the wedding, the bride's dress becomes a dress to wear to church.

The bride's coterie of attendants and friends (buddy girls, sisters, and sisters-in-law) can be identified by their dress color. It may match the bride's dress color, as has been common, or may be a complementary color, which has gained popularity in the past decade.

Susan chose a rich, dark green for her wedding dress. The same color would be worn by her mom, sisters, side sitters, Eck tenders, and buddy girls. Her nieces and youth group friends would wear her secondary color of a warm tan.

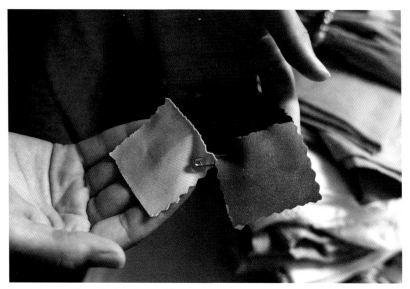

Rose's dress will be a dark, rich navy blue. Her side sitters, Eck tenders, sisters, sisters-in-law, and buddy girls will wear dresses made of a dark rose-colored fabric, and her young nieces will wear ivory rose. CHRISTY KAUFFMAN

Rose's "Look"

As someone who works in kitchen design, Rose is a visual thinker. She had a clear idea of the look she wanted for her wedding and how the dress colors and table accessories would complement one another. She chose a dark navy fabric that draped beautifully for her wedding dress and a dark rose for her twenty friends and sisters to wear.

She collected pink Depression glass dessert plates and other dishes and decorations to maintain her visual theme and adorn the tables, gift area, and Eck display.

Instead of the usual one or two dress colors for participants, Rose added a third color for her young nieces who helped collect gifts. The five little girls, looking sweet in their ivory pink dresses, were very excited to help.

Following the guidance of the apostle Paul in 1 Corinthians 11, Amish women and girls wear head coverings and do not cut their hair. When women and girls are at home, the head covering may be a kerchief; when out in public and in social settings, it's a white organdy or batiste cap.

Girls in some districts traditionally wear a black covering when attending church—and a white covering otherwise—until they marry. In such cases, a newly married bride switches from her black covering to a white covering directly after the wedding service and before the dinner. Girls in many church districts don't wear black coverings at all; the bride then maintains a white covering before and after her marriage.

Girls and unmarried young women wear white organdy capes and aprons over their dresses when they attend church. The white symbolizes purity. At a wedding, the bride and her side sitters wear white capes and

---

Capes and Aprons

Amish women and girls ages eight and up routinely wear capes and aprons over their solid-colored dresses. The apron's broad waistband is pinned closed at the waist; its skirt falls nearly to the dress hem, completely covering the front of the dress skirt and partially covering the back. The cape, which appears much like a vest, fits over the shoulders and is open at the sides and pinned to the waistband of the dress at the front and back. It covers the upper torso to maintain modesty. BETH OBERHOLTZER

aprons; the bride's single friends—as when attending a social event rather than a Sunday church service—wear capes that match the fabric of their dresses, and black aprons.

After marriage, a bride switches to wearing a colored cape and black apron for church and social events; around age thirty, she begins wearing a black cape instead of a colored cape.

A woman wears a white cape and apron for the last time at her wedding. She then carefully tucks them away—to next be worn at her funeral.

A bride-to-be may need to be creative in her search for the required wedding footwear. Black high-top shoes are routinely worn by older members of the church and by pastors' wives—but are not often found in a young woman's closet. She may survey her sisters and aunts to find a pair

High-top shoes are a must for the bride and groom, but styles vary. Rose's are a perfect combination of dressy and casual, which means they'll be suitable to wear beyond her wedding day. CHRISTY KAUFFMAN

Esther last wore this cape and apron when she married more than forty years ago. She will next wear it over a white dress to be buried. JOHN HERR

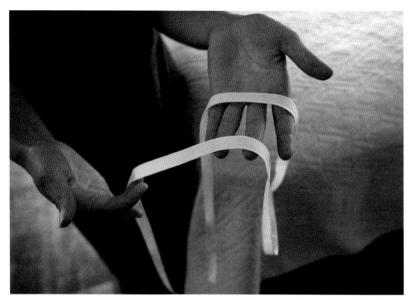

There is some variation in the width of the strings on a woman's head covering—from a quarter to three eighths to a half inch—depending on a district's tradition and trends among young people. Rose chose a half-inch width for her wedding covering. CHRISTY KAUFFMAN

to borrow. The groom, as well as the parents of the bride and groom, also wears high-top shoes to the wedding.

Even if some high-top shoes are trendy with the young women in a particular community, they're not likely the sort appropriate for a wedding. But Rose was thrilled to find the perfect amalgam—her new high-top black lace-ups were the right mix to satisfy her fashion-forward leanings while sedate and plain enough to not draw attention.

A good start for the couple

As in many families, inherited and household items are often collected in a girl's hope chest with thoughts of her future marriage. At her engagement, a bride and her mother review what else is needed.

The bride's parents customarily provide much of what is necessary to set up housekeeping when the bride and groom move into their new home. When a first daughter marries, her parents consult a list of what is traditionally supplied for the bride. It includes furniture, rugs, bed linens, blankets, comforters, and sewing and gardening supplies.

In generations past, the bride's mother worked for years to make multiple quilts for each daughter when she married. An all-white quilt was extra special and often graced the guest room bed. The practice of giving quilts has since dwindled in popularity. Couples have a broad variety of bedding to choose among—and it may or may not include handmade quilts.

Heirloom seeds preserved by previous generations help fill the garden with tea leaves, peas, tomatoes, and more, plus a variety of gorgeous flowers.

Food for hundreds

An Amish mother is accustomed to feeding lots of people—from her immediate family to her teens' youth gatherings to her entire church district

Sallie grew red and yellow bell peppers, which she cubed and pickled to decorate the coleslaw that would be served at her youngest daughter's wedding. CHRISTY KAUFFMAN

after a service. However, four or five hundred guests for two meals may strain anyone's limits.

It is suspected that a Lancaster County Amish wedding couldn't even take place without a traditional dinner menu that includes roast (chicken and stuffing), mashed potatoes and gravy, creamed cooked celery, and coleslaw. Additional dishes for dinner and those for supper vary. Each recipe for hundreds includes a dizzying volume of ingredients.

When the bride and her mother have worked out the foods that will be served, the task of matching needs with sources begins. Where do the ingredients come from? Who will make each dish? Where should we buy the doughnuts?

Spring planting in the garden can include produce to be used at a fall wedding. Sallie grew ten heads of cabbage to be shredded for coleslaw. Her red bell pepper plants yielded dozens of peppers to pickle and preserve—they would be scattered over the top of the bowls of coleslaw. The hundreds of potatoes she grew ended up in kettles, cooked and mashed with butter and milk. Tomatoes were turned into a tangy barbecue sauce for the chicken at supper.

Though the heads are tiny in August, this cabbage will be ready for an October wedding. The celery, ready to harvest in October, was protected from the sun by covered wooden frames to maintain a light green color and sweet flavor. **LEFT:** CHRISTY KAUFFMAN, **RIGHT:** BETH OBERHOLTZER

With an eye toward upcoming weddings, family gardens may also include extra rows of celery, carrots, string beans, and corn. Katie Ann froze twenty-five quarts of shelled peas for her daughter's wedding—around a quarter to a third cup per person—totaling more than thirty thousand peas!

Friends and relatives are frequently enlisted to make pies and cookies or other snacks. Local vendors and warehouse stores are shopped for additional ingredients and provisions. Food that is partially or completely prepared ahead of time is kept in rented refrigerators and freezers. The same appliances are used to store leftovers until they are given to helpers, family members, or those in need. Other leftovers may be frozen for future use.

Even when a meal is served in three shifts, with dishes washed in between, hundreds of serving dishes, dinner dishes, cups, and sets of flatware are needed. Married friends and relatives of the bride who have a particular cooking assignment bring the kettles, roast pans, and tools related to their job. They mark all the items with their names so the pieces go home with them at the end of the day.

Instead of securing items piecemeal from multiple suppliers, many households go to outside vendors who can provide the whole range of necessities in one package. The practice of renting several refrigerators and stoves to place in basements or workshops has, in some cases, given way to renting a wedding or utility trailer to park on-site that contains those appliances and more. And given the huge amounts of food that are prepared and must be safely stored for several days, a cooler trailer can serve as a giant refrigerator.

Help freely offered

When Katie Ann heard that her niece was getting married in November, the question wasn't whether she would be asked to help, but simply what her job would be. In addition to having hosted their two oldest daughters' weddings, she and her husband had the experience to perform any chore needed. Perhaps they would be asked to be Forgeher—guiding guests to their seats, directing room setup, and maintaining order throughout the

Tasks for Relatives and Good Friends of the Bride's Family

	Siblings of the bride and good friends of the bride and groom	
	SINGLE SIBLINGS AND FRIENDS	MARRIED COUPLES
In the weeks before the wedding	Make new dresses; make or buy new suits	
	Help clean and paint	4 Eck tender couples selected to serve the bridal party; women plan foods to serve on the wedding day
A few days before the wedding	Help wash windows, clean floors	Eck tenders finalize plans for food and how it will be displayed in the Eck
Day before 50 or more people arrive to help prepare	Sweep walks, rake driveway and yard, final touch-ups Help with food preparation Make sure all gathering areas are ready for guests Prepare barn and property for guests' horses and buggies Siblings, single or married, help out wherever needed	Eck tenders set up Eck table and begin to arrange treat and food gifts on display; prepare some foods Food preparation
Wedding day All the bride's relatives arrive expecting to be put to work where needed	2 side sitters (attendants) each for bride and groom 6–10 boys and young married men serve as hostlers throughout the day and perform chores in the late afternoon	Eck tenders prepare and serve special foods for the bridal party throughout the day Food preparation and cleanup Wrap doughnuts after dinner Wash dishes 10 serve Big Table supper 4 serve Family Table supper 4 serve Small Table supper

Aunts and uncles of the bride; church members and close neighbors of the bride's family

COUPLES	WOMEN	MEN
Help when see what needs to be done	2 paper ladies plan with bride's mother	Draw diagram of additions or buildings and site map
		Are available as needed
Help pick up ordered items	Make pies, cakes, doughnuts	Help with construction of
	Help write out recipes and	addition or erection of
Forgeher (ushers) make sure	organize ingredients	wedding house
they know seating	Make dressing for salad	Deliver bench wagons
arrangements and	Help clean	Move in cooking equipment
schedule		Fetch chickens for roast
Scrub potatoes	Help with final cleaning	Finalize construction and cleanup
Dice bread for stuffing	2 make lunch or brunch	of property
Fill water jugs	2 or 3 chest ladies organize	Set up benches for service
	dishes for table and	Trial run of transitioning benches
Table waiters organize dishes	serving	to tables
for dinner	Prep chicken; 20 women each	
Forgeher make sure council	take two home to roast	Older men chop celery for
room is set up	Prep celery	creamed celery
	Make salads; boil eggs	
	Prepare fruit for salad	
4 Forgeher direct guests	2 serve as paper ladies	15 transition benches to tables
throughout the day	3 in charge of dish chests	2 supply hot water for washing
4 make roast	Return roasted chicken with	dishes
3 make mashed potatoes	meat removed from bone	
	2 make cooked celery	1 sweeps barn in morning and
10 serve Big Table dinner	2 make gravy	afternoon
4 serve Family Table dinner	3 make coleslaw	2 tend lights
4 serve Small Table dinner		1 tends trash
	2 tend dishes	1 keeps water jugs filled
2 to 4 make and serve	1 or 2 hang out tea towels	1 maintains heaters and
afternoon snack	4 make forenoon snack	woodstoves
2 prepare supper dessert	2 make fruit salad or trays	
1 or 2 wrap doughnuts		Are available as needed
All aunts and uncles who have	2 tend portable toilets and	
not been assigned other	wash stations	
tasks wash dishes	2 fix leftover food for groom's	
	parents, grandparents, sick	
Prepare food basket for family	neighbors	
and those in need		
6 cook supper (usually parents'	6 maintain coffee all day	
buddies)	2 tidy kitchen in house	
	throughout day	

The helpers at Elam and Mary Ann's wedding received gifts of wooden boxes created by the groom out of tobacco lath and filled with a tea towel, water bottle, carpenter's pencil, and handmade soap. Jay and Rose gave glasses engraved with their names to 108 of their closest friends. **LEFT:** BETH OBERHOLTZER, **RIGHT:** CHRISTY KAUFFMAN

day. Maybe Katie Ann would be one of the dozen or more cooks, or the paper lady who directs the cooks and others in their duties.

The bride's family is responsible for purchasing the considerable amount of food—or the ingredients to make it—necessary to feed four or five hundred; they rent or borrow equipment, appliances, dishes, tents, and other wedding gear. They do not, however, hire help. The roughly 150 people needed to perform jobs from ushering to cooking to serving to cleaning up are all relatives and friends from the bride's side of the family—and all are assigned their tasks by the bride's mother.

There's a sense of camaraderie and purpose in working together to make the day special. It might be a little tricky for the mother of the bride to determine who is available with skills that fit each job while also making sure that one aunt isn't selected as paper lady at multiple weddings while another is repeatedly on portable toilet cleaning duty.

Gift-giving at Amish weddings does not flow in only one direction. The bride and her family present tokens of their regard and appreciation to the friends of the couple as well as attendants and family members who serve on the wedding day. When the bride and groom spend time with their friends on the afternoon of the wedding, they also hand out treats.

The approximately two hundred women guests at Abram and Susan's wedding were each given a tiny potted palm grown from plants that the family tended over the summer. Wedding cooks received larger versions of the plants. Each male guest was given a hoof pick, and the hostlers were treated to root beer. **TOP:** BETH OBERHOLTZER, **LEFT:** JOHN HERR

Susan and her mother tended a small forest of bella palm plants on their porch throughout the summer, maintaining them carefully so they'd be ready to give with thanks to the aunts and uncles who helped at the November wedding. Newlyweds also pass favors out to friends and other wedding helpers. Personalized mugs and glasses are popular gifts. One bride delighted her buddy girls with specially flavored vinegar in decorative bottles. When guests leave a wedding in the evening, the newlyweds ask them to sign the guest book and to take along a favor such as a personalized pencil, bookmark, ruler, or pen.

Key volunteers

An Amish wedding calls on the labor and cooking skills of a whole community. The menu and schedule may be set, but months of preparation and many helping hands are employed before, during, and after the event. There are two main meals to make and serve—plus the afternoon table and snacks offered throughout the day. Seating and tables must be arranged, then rearranged, depending on what's happening when. And there are hundreds of people (and dozens of horses) to manage.

Helping with a wedding is viewed as an honor and is taken very seriously. There is satisfaction to be found working with others and enjoying their company. Katherine explained: "I don't have a favorite job—I like them all. But I wouldn't want to do the same one all the time."

The bride's uncles, aunts, and older married siblings automatically show up at the bride's home and are put to work the day before, the day of, and the day after the wedding. Close church people also rally around.

An outsider can imagine how daunting any of the jobs might be. But guests in the community have helped at numerous weddings and attended many more. The day's routine becomes second nature. Older and younger folks work together as a team; the older teach the younger. As the younger ones gain years and experience, they mentor the next generation.

There are three major management teams that keep an Amish wedding on track: paper ladies, Forgeher, and Eck tenders. In addition, the hostlers direct parking, tend the horses, and do other chores.

Paper ladies

One or two women, often sisters of the bride's mother, oversee "things." Though sometimes called head cooks, their job is supervisory. "Paper ladies" or "list ladies" can be identified early on by the bundle of papers they have in hand—long lists, provided by the bride's mother, of jobs with the names of people who are assigned to fill them. They make detailed plans with the bride's mother well ahead of time. It's vital to "make sure you know everything," Leah said. "Ask, ask, ask."

"Paper ladies do everything the day of the wedding."

Paper ladies make sure the assigned cooks for multiple meals have everything they need to do their jobs—ingredients, pots, pans, dishes, utensils. They keep an eye on those tasked with washing dishes, filling water jugs, maintaining lights, making coffee, and taking care of the toilets. And they make sure that cooks and servers stay on schedule.

Linda Mae's aunt reviews information from Linda Mae's mom in preparation to serve as a paper lady at her niece's upcoming wedding in a few weeks. BETH OBERHOLTZER

It is vital to know where everything is ahead of time. Though the mother of the bride has provided detailed instructions, she cannot be concerned with questions on the wedding day.

- As paper lady, Katie Ann had a specific directive from the bride's mom to put strawberries in the fruit salad for dinner and on top of the cake for supper. The afternoon of the wedding, she realized they didn't have enough strawberries, so she sent her husband out to the store for more. The bride's mom never knew about it, but she'd provided cash for emergencies.

- The only thing Ada remembers about being a paper lady at one wedding was not being able to find part of the coffee pot—and coffee was essential. "We eventually found it on a high shelf, but not knowing was awful," she said.

- Leah was a paper lady for her niece's wedding and found it quite stressful. She said, "This is the best advice I received as a paper lady: Never say 'I don't know.' Say 'I will look.' Then go and find what they need."

A vital skill for a paper lady is organization—and it helps if it is an innate trait. A woman in her forties or fifties is in her prime as a paper lady. She's old enough to have attended many weddings and certainly helped at them yet young enough to work hard. Though not every woman is naturally a paper lady, each gets a turn. A newly minted paper lady or someone who is a little scattered is paired with someone calm and experienced.

Women who are asked to be paper ladies nearly always accept—unless, like Elizabeth, they are getting into their seventies and think the younger women are better suited to it. She suggested that "maybe an older woman will make gravy or keep up the coffee all day."

"Chest ladies" oversee the dishes and often act as second in command to paper ladies. They oversee the organization of the dishes (which are likely transported on a rolling rack rather than in an actual chest) before, during, and the day after the wedding day. They count all pieces when the dishes arrive and when the dishes are packed for return to make sure nothing is missing.

The Forgeher direct guests to where they may gather in the morning prior to the wedding. The married men talk together outside in front of the horse barn (at left) while the unmarried "boys" gather inside in the lower level at the center of the horse barn. JOHN HERR

Forgeher

Generally, aunts and uncles of the bride (four couples total), are invited to serve as *Forgeher* (ushers). The mother and father of the bride each select two of their siblings and spouses. If the aunts and uncles are getting up in years, the bride's married siblings serve instead. So depending on stamina and skills, the Forgeher may range in age from their twenties to their mid-sixties.

Two key assets for Forgeher are being able to quickly identify members of the bride's and groom's families and being comfortable with telling people what to do and when. Their job is essentially crowd control on the day of the wedding—seating for the service, eating, and singing. The men on the Forgeher teams direct the men; the women direct the women. Forgeher are routinely advised to stay calm. "There's no use getting all worked up," said Sarah. Esther likes the position of Forgeher. She likes to be out and interacting. "I enjoy being with the people," she said.

Eck tenders

Three or four married couples from the bride's side of the family, often siblings or close friends of the couple, are invited to serve as Eck tenders. The Eck tenders are essentially dedicated attendants to the bride and groom for the day, not only meeting but anticipating the needs of the couple. For example, "It looks like you need more brown butter for your

It is common for engaged girls to collect dishes and decorations and maintain a growing display in the months before their weddings. Eck tenders at a recent wedding laid the table for the bride and groom with lace runners, cloth napkins, a tiered serving stand, decorative candles, new flatware, and vintage saucers. CHRISTY KAUFFMAN

potatoes. I'll go get some." The women on the team are more likely to understand the food and decoration tasks that need to be done, and hence they take the lead and direct their husbands.

A few weeks before the wedding, the women Eck tenders visit the bride to receive instructions. They review and wash the bride's new china to make sure they have place settings for the bride and groom and their side sitters plus serving dishes for the various foods. The bride explains what special menu items she'd like and gives the recipes. They organize and put the dishes in order and mark what each will be used for.

The Eck tenders are on call all day to serve the bridal couple, mostly making and presenting food. They perform other tasks as well, such as organizing the Eck gifts brought to the wedding and passing out treats to close relatives during meals. Serving in this way is not burdensome; Eck tenders find great enjoyment working with and for their friends.

Hostlers

When most of the four hundred or more wedding guests travel by horse and buggy, there may be up to a hundred carriages to park and horses to tend. Older folks might hire a driver with a car or van if the trip is over fifteen miles, but youth, who are likely less pressed for time, may drive up to twenty-five miles to a wedding.

Eight to ten boys in their young teens and several young married church men in their twenties take care of the horses. The boys are often quietly thrilled to be selected to serve as hostlers. Depending on the age of the bride, the younger workers may be her brothers, nephews, or cousins. If she has been a teacher, she may ask her older boy students, around twelve or thirteen years old, to do the honors. Sometimes sons of coworkers or young coworkers themselves are asked to serve.

Hostlers arrive early on the wedding day to be ready to tend the guests' horses. JOHN HERR

Shades of Meaning in Men's Hats

Black felt
Flat top
2.5-inch brim

Straw
Flat top
2.5-inch brim

Black felt
Telescope top
3-inch brim

Black felt
Telescope top
3.5-inch brim

To the casual observer, Amish men and boys simply wear black hats or straw hats—black hats to church in the cool months, straw hats to church in the summer. And generally straw hats for work and other outdoor activities year-round.

But there is so much more nuance than that. Differences among hats are based on the wearer's age, the occasion, his marital status and that of his family members, and his position in the church.

Since each male member of the household has three or more hats, things can get confusing. There may be the Sunday felt hat, the Sunday straw hat, the knockabout straw hat, and the everyday straw hat.

Sallie is the mother of four sons, now mostly grown. She said, "*I was always buying straw hats! Maybe the dog ate it. Maybe the bull got it in the meadow. Maybe it got lost or mixed up with someone else's.*"

Toddler boys through age eight wear flat-top felt hats with 2.5-inch brims to church in cold weather and straw hats with the same size brim in warm weather.

At age nine or a few days before, it's an important rite of passage for a dad to buy his son a telescope-top (crown) felt hat with a 2.75- to 3-inch brim to replace his little-boy-style flat-top hat.

Youth from age nine until marriage often wear felt and straw hats with 3-inch brims. Some older youth in more conservative areas move to a 3.5-inch brim and continue wearing that size until well into their married years.

Youth attending their baptism services, usually in their late teens or early twenties, wear telescope-top felt hats with 3.5-inch brims. Afterward, some switch back to hats with 3-inch brims.

Young men in some areas wear hats only to church and to weddings.

Straw for church
Flat top
3.5-inch brim

Black felt
Flat top
3.5-inch brim

Straw for work
Flat top
3.5-inch brim

JOHN HERR

A groom wears a telescope-top felt hat with 3.5-inch brim to his wedding (the same as he wore at baptism). Afterward, he might switch back to wearing a hat with a 3-inch brim to church.

Some married men, after four or five years of marriage, and following the custom of men in their church district, begin wearing telescope-top felt hats with 3.5-inch brims to church.

Married men, upon the marriage of their first child, begin wearing flat-top felt hats with 3.5-inch brims.

Ministers, bishops, and deacons begin wearing flat-top felt hats with 4-inch brims immediately after being ordained.

Not everyone's life unfolds the same way. A man may be unmarried, or married with no children, or have only unmarried children. If so, his hat wardrobe changes on a timeline similar to that of his contemporaries.

HAT BANDS

The width of a black hat's ribbon band has meaning also. The most common three sizes are half inch, three quarters inch, and one inch. The wider grosgrain ribbons likely adorn the wider-brimmed hats of older men.

STRAW HATS

- The brim size of a wearer's straw hat generally stays consistent with his felt hat brim size, though there are differences based on personal taste.

- A work hat's band may be cloth ribbon, electrical tape, or simply a knotted shoelace.

- It's not unusual, in the workaday world or with little boys, to see straw hats repaired with duct tape. Some straw hats are worn so hard their brims are completely gone and the hat is just a crown.

- Many men routinely replace their Sunday straw hat with a new one each year and demote the good hat to serve as a work hat.

99

The groom and his family

Fanny's kitchen table is the command center from which she directs most aspects of family life. One September afternoon, it was covered with mounds of black quilted fabric. A few weeks later, beef heart rested on a tray while its companion tongue boiled on the stove. They had just slaughtered a beef cow and were having some of the ground beef made into beef sticks.

Fanny is the mother of ten: two sons and three daughters are married with children, and three sons and two daughters still live at home. Arlen, her sixth and middle child, would be getting married in early December. The mother of Miriam, his intended, was awash in lists as she planned food and scheduled a multitude of volunteers in preparation for her daughter's wedding that would take place the first Tuesday in December.

What the groom wears

Though the bride's mother assumed the bulk of the planning, Fanny had responsibilities as the groom's mother. When she made winter coats for her husband and three younger sons, she also sewed four winter coats to send with Arlen into his marriage. She also made six sets of shirts and pants and two pairs of suit pants. They bought the suitcoat and vest from an Amish seamstress.

"That's enough clothes for him until his bride can make what he needs."

Women in previous generations sewed all clothing for the family as a matter of course. In recent years, the specialized tailoring that is required for a man's *Mutse* (Sunday coat) and *Wescht* (vest) is frequently outsourced to in-home seamstresses who sell directly to customers or through specialized Amish clothing stores.

A groom's wedding suit is a new and pristine version of a standard black Sunday suit. Typically made of black polyester suiting fabric, the jacket has a deep V-neck with no lapels; the pieced back has a single vent opening in the lower part of the seam. The cut of the vest front matches the cut of the jacket, and both close with hooks. Under the vest and jacket

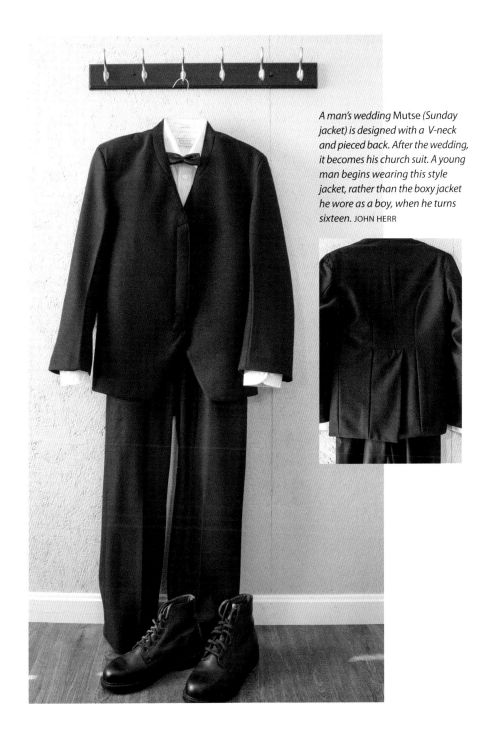

A man's wedding Mutse *(Sunday jacket) is designed with a V-neck and pieced back. After the wedding, it becomes his church suit. A young man begins wearing this style jacket, rather than the boxy jacket he wore as a boy, when he turns sixteen.* JOHN HERR is a white long-sleeved collared dress shirt. The groom's button suspenders secure his black broadfall pants.

Lending formality to the occasion, the groom, his side sitters, and perhaps the Eck tenders wear black clip-on bow ties. A white handkerchief is tucked out of sight.

"Don't forget the Schlupp (bow tie)!"

Like the bride, the groom wears high-top shoes for the wedding. After that, he will return to wearing his low-topped black shoes for church. If he is ordained to the ministry, he'll begin wearing high-top shoes. Otherwise, twenty or so years later when his contemporaries also make the change, he'll pull the high-tops out of his closet and begin wearing them to church. This may correspond to when his first son or daughter joins a youth group or becomes engaged to be married.

To top off the outfit, the groom dons a black telescope-top hat (also known as a telescope-crown hat) with a three-and-a-half-inch brim. Depending on his community and preferences, he has likely been wearing a hat with a three-inch brim and may have last worn the hat with the three-and-a-half-inch brim for his baptism.

After the wedding, the groom's wedding suit becomes his Sunday suit—without the bow tie.

Provisions from family

Along with supplying multiple sets of clothing, the groom's parents are expected to provide the couple with a variety of housekeeping items. These things, in addition to what the bride's family provides and wedding guests give as gifts, will likely carry the couple for some years. The furniture is given to the couple when they move into their own home rather than immediately upon marriage, when they are still living with the bride's family.

The groom and his family also need to think about wedding-day favors. A few generations ago, young married men gave cigars to their friends. These days, they'll more likely pass out beef sticks and a variety of candies and gum. While Arlen's parents had slaughtered a beef cow for their butcher to make beef sticks for the groom's young friends to enjoy, fewer Amish families today raise beef cattle. It is now common to buy the beef sticks from a butcher. A groom need only choose the flavor or two he wants from among the sweet, spicy, cheesy, maple, barbecue and other options offered.

Choice of buggy horse

An important consideration for a young man getting married is transportation. He has likely had his own horse and buggy since his mid-teens, and they will go into the marriage with him. But the kind of horse a young man chooses—likely one with spirit and verve—may not be ideal for a family man.

When dating, he might have driven his buggy horse more than twenty miles to visit his girlfriend, then home again, every weekend for a year or more. That gives a high-strung horse plenty of exercise, which helps keep it calm. After the man marries, his horse no longer gets the regular long-distance workout and can be a challenge for his new bride to handle. The couple will then buy a more sedate horse, which is especially welcome when they add children to the family.

FIVE

The Essential Wedding Menu

The bride's relatives help out by roasting chickens the day before the wedding. BETH OBERHOLTZER

The throughline of an Amish wedding, in addition to celebrating a couple's marriage, is the wealth of food offered. During the daylong event, the equivalent of three meals is served: dinner, afternoon table, and supper—plus a forenoon snack for workers and snacks for all guests throughout the day.

Since guests do not respond to a wedding invitation indicating whether they will attend, hosts must make their best guess about how many people will come and how much food to prepare.

There is an art to anticipating how many guests to expect and estimating how much they will eat. Sarah explained that more weddings take place in the fall than in the spring, so guests may have to choose among weddings to attend on a given day—thus, fewer guests will attend than invited. But since guests may have gone a long stretch without enjoying the traditional wedding meal, they will eat heartily. "It's a treat to have a wedding dinner again," she said.

Later in the season they may find the same fare a little less tempting. Since there are fewer weddings in the spring, more invited guests will attend, but they may eat less. Sarah said, "Later in the season, eating the meal isn't so special."

Laura, who made weddings for three of her daughters, is less concerned about the numbers. She said that their hosting space is flexible and that they make plenty of food for the number of guests invited, so having the exact count ahead isn't necessary. They routinely give away or freeze the leftovers.

One of the Forgeher is assigned to "count plates" at each meal seating—which is considerably easier than counting heads—for an actual number of attendees. The mother of the bride keeps careful records of how much of each dish was made and how much was left over and uses the information to plan subsequent weddings and advise friends.

The main dishes served at an Amish wedding dinner have remained the same for generations. Without pause, Grandma Stoltzfus, in her eighties, could name what she and her husband had at their wedding dinner more than sixty years ago. And she had the same thing just last fall at her grandson's wedding. The meal *always* includes roast (chicken mixed with stuffing and baked in a roast pan), cooked celery, mashed potatoes and gravy, and coleslaw with sweet-and-sour peppers. There are also rolls with butter and jelly or cinnamon butter, fruit, often pie, and coffee. Platters or tiered stands hold a variety of cookies and the favored selection of blueberry, glazed, and cream-filled doughnuts.

Upon hearing of an engagement, women friends and family ask, "What do you want me to make?" The bride's mother assigns eight women to each bring 125 cookies. There are usually 250 chocolate chip cookies (always the most popular) and six other kinds. Some women have cookie specialties that they're often asked to make. "My cousin Lizzie makes these terribly good nut cookies," Sarah said. Sometimes there are exotic offerings like chocolate-coated peanut butter crackers or chocolate-dipped whoopie pies. Cupcakes may be offered instead of some of the cookies, but experienced cooks think that may be just a temporary trend.

Even when a family is committed to healthy eating, a wedding is a time to indulge. "No one wants to serve just fiber balls," said Susie.

The modern couple often prefers a fresh fruit salad rather than the customary home-canned applesauce or peaches and pears. A variety of pies may be served: chocolate shoofly, vanilla, yogurt, peanut butter, pecan, or pumpkin. This follows the fall wedding tradition when a family used what they had in the cellar.

The bride and her mother generally plan additional side dishes and desserts for dinner. And since there is no set menu for the food at afternoon table or at supper, they have free rein—as long as whatever is selected can be efficiently prepared and served to hundreds.

Organized by the bride's mother and managed by the paper ladies, "food people" form specialized teams to make the main dinner dishes of roast, celery, mashed potatoes, gravy, and coleslaw. The food preparation is assigned to married members of the bride's family, family friends, and church people. Their jobs are given ahead of time, which explains why a couple walking to a neighbor's wedding may be seen carrying a shiny twelve-quart kettle.

Working together

Cooking for a wedding is a huge amount of work, but it's fun to work together—and is a social investment. As is commonly understood, "We do it for each other." Experienced workers are paired with younger workers so the next generation can grow into the jobs. Some brides' mothers are so detail-oriented that they carefully assign joint jobs to people whose strengths complement each other and who will particularly enjoy each other's company.

Every cook has their own way of making things, so it is important for the mother of the bride to provide the exact recipe she wants used. But Sarah makes sure she's careful in her wording. "We know how we want it to be, but we don't want to be bossy." Even so, there can be differences of opinion. When preparing the raw chicken to roast, is it best to rub it with melted butter or to dip the whole chicken in melted butter?

When making brown-butter noodles for supper, is it best to pour the brown butter over the top after the noodles are cooked and drained or to pour the brown butter in the water the noodles are cooked in?

"We have to have the grace to come together when we disagree."

Linda Mae's aunts help dress the chickens that her groom-to-be slaughtered for their wedding dinner. BETH OBERHOLTZER

Food people are keenly aware of the level of tension felt by many mothers of the bride. Even though the mother of the bride is not to be bothered with any questions or problems on the day of the wedding, an effort is made to assure her that things are going well. The bride and groom are not likely thinking about what they're eating, but the food servers make sure they present the most beautiful representation of each dish at the parents' table.

Roast

Part of the lore of the "Amish roast" (*Rooscht*) is the groom-to-be's relationship with the chicken. Actually, thirty-six to forty chickens. The bride's family traditionally raised them, and the day before the wedding, the groom would slaughter the chickens and the women would dress them. As many families moved off the farm and commercially raised poultry became the norm, the custom waned. It was much easier to buy the chicken than to deal with the messy business of blood and guts and feathers. Most families turned to ordering their chickens from the poultry dealer.

Families in some communities, however, maintain the tradition of raising their own chickens. A few weeks before his wedding to Linda Mae, Abner got up bright and early and beheaded thirty-six hefty broiler chickens that Linda Mae's parents had raised for the occasion. He dipped them in scalding water and turned them over to Linda Mae's aunts, who swiftly plucked them, removed their insides, and singed off the pinfeathers. They reserved the hearts, livers, and gizzards to mix in with the dinner roast.

Some modern couples have begun to raise their own chickens. They can carefully control the environment and diet to make sure the chickens have been humanely treated and that the meat is free of antibiotics. They value serving a healthier chicken to their guests.

Roast people

Several days before the wedding, the bride's mother lays bread cubes out to dry on clean sheets. It's virtually always white bread to allow the flavor of the chicken to shine.

On the day before the wedding, the "roast people" (four couples—usually two older and two younger) make the stuffing and fill the chickens for roasting. They spread the dried bread cubes out on a new plastic tarp the size of two bedsheets. The four men stationed at the corners take turns rolling the contents, lifting and lowering the tarp one corner at a time, to mix when each new batch of ingredients is added. The women help the men by warning them if the stuffing-in-process is in danger of sailing off the sides of the plastic sheet.

The women who work at the bride's home, whatever their task, bring their own roast pans with lids and pans clearly marked with their names. They leave at the end of the day with each roast pan containing two stuffed chickens to roast at their own home before the wedding. If needed, some women take four chickens.

Esther took home two chickens and roasted them the day before her niece's wedding. She returned the meat, broth, filling, and skin on the wedding morning, and the roast people mixed the ingredients together. BETH OBERHOLTZER

The next day, on the morning of the wedding, the women return with the cooked meat completely picked from the bones, with the skin and broth reserved. Each woman who is part of a roast couple brings her specialized tools, including a paring knife and kitchen shears to snip the meat into small pieces. What size chicken pieces are best? Melvin has a firm opinion: "Don't cut the pieces too small; I don't want it already chewed."

The roast people combine the cooked chicken and stuffing with the remaining uncooked stuffing, once again using the huge tarp for mixing. The mixture is placed back into the same roast pans and baked.

"After a day making roast, everybody's friends."

The first three or four roast pans are put in the oven early in the morning, timed to come out of the oven as a mid-morning snack for the hostlers and other workers (forty or fifty people). After that, the goal is to have a dozen roasts ready to go just as the first seating of guests is ready to eat dinner—around noon. Is the roast usually browned? David prefers it a little crispy: "Roast isn't roast unless it's roasted."

Celery

To the chagrin of some traditionalists, celery does not feature as prominently in some Amish weddings as it did in the past. Yes, cooked celery is a vital part of the noon meal—and celery is ground and mixed with the stuffing for roast and finely chopped for the cabbage dish. But vases of celery hearts gracing the tables throughout the day—lauded as beautiful decorations and crisp palate cleansers—aren't seen as necessary for some brides.

In years past, when engaged couples were secretive about their wedding plans, the sight of a long row of covered celery in the family garden indicated that a wedding would be coming in the fall. Celery that is covered as it grows results in stalks that are a light yellow green with a sweeter flavor. A family with generous garden space may grow their own celery; others order it from their grocer.

Roast (*Rooscht*)

Yields 17 pans of roast
Serves approximately 400 people

34 (7- to 7½-pound) broiler chickens
34 gallons bread cubes, or 20 loaves bread, cubed
25 pounds butter, divided
68 eggs
15 tablespoons salt, plus additional for sprinkling over chicken
 2 cups black pepper, plus more as desired
 5 gallons chopped celery, then ground (about 16 bunches), juices reserved
 1 tablespoon red pepper, or to taste

Day before wedding:

Remove and reserve the giblets from the chickens, including heart and liver.

On a large, new plastic tarp, dump all the bread cubes. Brown 17 pounds of the butter and sprinkle over the bread cubes. Tumble together until well mixed.

Beat the eggs, then add the 15 tablespoons salt and half of the black pepper to the eggs. Pour the egg mixture over the bread cubes. Mix until all the ingredients are combined.

Dump the ground celery on top of the bread cubes and mix. Reserve the juice to pour on the roast the next day.

Melt the remaining 8 pounds of butter in two 12-quart kettles. Dip each chicken in the melted butter and sprinkle with salt. Stuff the chickens loosely, about 2 quarts of stuffing for each chicken. Place two chickens in each roast pan to send home with the helpers to roast, pick apart, and bring back the next day.

Refrigerate the remaining stuffing.

Cook the livers and hearts (giblets) by simmering. Refrigerate and save for the next day.

Day of wedding:

Grind the cold giblets.

The chickens will be returned in their roast pan with a pile of meat, a pile of skin, a pile of stuffing, and the broth in a plastic container. Cut the chicken into pieces using scissors. Don't make the pieces too small. Grind the skin with a hand-turn meat grinder. Give the broth to the gravy people.

Add the chicken, cooked stuffing, and ground giblets to the refrigerated (uncooked) stuffing and mix together.

Wash and dry the roast pans. Spray the pans with baking spray. Fill each roast pan with roast. Pour the reserved celery juice around the edges of each pan of roast (to keep the bottom and sides from getting too brown), and top with ground skin. Add more pepper on top of the roast once it is in the pans. Sprinkle a little red pepper on top. Cover with foil.

Roast at 375°F. Place two pans of roast on the single bottom rack of each oven, one resting directly on top of the other and placed at an angle so they fit in. Stir just once during the first hour of baking. Swap pans in the oven to keep the bottom pans from burning or becoming too brown. Roast takes about 2 hours to bake. Remove from the roast pans and keep warm in an insulated ice chest until time to serve.

Use a saucer in each hand to scoop the roast to transfer into prewarmed serving platters.

On the day before the wedding, the bride and groom and their side sitters have the job of washing the celery bunches before passing the ribs along to be chopped.

Since workers often bring their own tools, it's important to keep track of them. One wife is careful with her favorite knife and cutting board. "I keep them out of sight (so no one else borrows them) until my husband needs them," she said.

Men who have reached a certain age—who are no longer up to the exertions of hauling benches and chairs—naturally gravitate to the kitchen table. There, the older men gather to chop celery and catch up on family news. They cut the celery into three-eighths-inch to half-inch pieces for the cooked celery and a finer cut for the coleslaw. The job is done when four twelve-quart kettles are filled to heaping for the cooked celery and five quarts for the coleslaw.

Celery people

On the morning of the wedding, the "celery people" (two women) take over. The sauce includes generous amounts of butter, white sugar, brown sugar, and sweetened condensed milk. Since tending the kettles doesn't require heavy lifting, this may be a job for older women.

Older men frequently have the job of chopping celery on the day before the wedding. Celery is featured in three of the main wedding dishes.
BETH OBERHOLTZER

The celery needs a substantial amount of cooking time before adding the sauce and cooking it further. Emma and Mary talked about the time they made the celery and were quite pleased with how the sauce turned out. But things somehow went wrong. One stove burner was turned up too high, and it scorched a kettle of celery, making it inedible. They thought maybe they had been too pleased with themselves.

Cooked Celery (*Koched Selleri*)

Yields 4 12-quart kettles
1 kettle serves about 100 people

4 heaping kettles' full chopped celery (about 50 bunches)

For each kettle:

- 2 cups granulated sugar
- 2 tablespoons salt
- ½ pound (2 sticks) butter
- 2 cups water
- 3½ tablespoons apple cider vinegar, divided
- 2 tablespoons flour
- 1 cup brown sugar
- 1 (12-ounce) can evaporated milk
- 1 cup heavy cream

Add the sugar, salt, butter, water, and 2½ tablespoons of the vinegar to each kettle of celery. Simmer for about 2 hours or until soft, stirring often.

Mix together the flour, brown sugar, evaporated milk, heavy cream, and remaining 1 tablespoon vinegar.

Add the flour mixture to the cooked celery. Pour it in all at one time—fast. Stir until well mixed. Heat but do not boil after mixture is added.

In Verna's recipe, she notes how celery people can fine-tune each stage of cooking based on what's going on outside the kitchen. They turn the burners on high when the celery is started in the morning before the church service begins (around seven thirty). After workers are served a snack (at eight thirty) while service continues, the cooks reduce the heat to medium-low. When the couple stands to marry during the service (at about ten thirty), the cooks check and stir the celery. After the couple is married and during the final sermon (toward eleven thirty), the cooks add the flour mixture and heat it through. Then at noon it's ready to serve.

Potatoes and gravy

Potato people

Making mashed potatoes for an Amish wedding is a multi-person job. It's one thing to whip up a bowl of potatoes to feed a family of six and a whole other thing to feed hundreds. Three couples, "potato people," are given the task of preparing the mashed potatoes. When Mervin and Katherine are assigned to potatoes, they bring their own tools the morning of the wedding: a twelve-quart kettle, a power drill with mixing attachment, a paring knife, a peeler, and aprons for them both. Because it's such a big job, church ladies may be called on to peel the potatoes if they're not working elsewhere.

Church people may be called on to help the potato people by peeling hundreds of potatoes.
BETH OBERHOLTZER

Potato people are married couples. The women cook the potatoes and supervise while the men provide the muscle and power tools to mash them. BETH OBERHOLTZER

In generations past, potatoes were cooked in big iron kettles, corralled within cloth bags (flour sacks or, later, pillowcases) tied closed with cotton twine. Now there's a row of stainless steel kettles on stovetops.

Jacob remembers the strength and stamina needed when he used a coil-style hand masher years ago, so he was glad to see his son put his battery-operated power drill to work. In an improvement over the common mixer attachment, a new stainless steel beater was invented to fit into the drill for mashing lots of potatoes. It has a longer neck and narrow blades, so, as Martha said, it's "not so splattery."

In a husband-and-wife potato team, the wife cooks the potatoes to the right consistency, then turns the kettle over to her husband. He fits his power drill with its mashing attachment and gets to work. She adds the milk and butter and stands by to add more milk if needed—especially if the potatoes are dry because of a dry summer.

An enterprising Amish man, no doubt having been a potato person more than once, recently invented a high-powered masher called a "tater turbo." It consists of a twelve-quart flat-bottomed container with a clear lid. A shaft with multiple blades fits into the center. The operator attaches a power drill to the shaft and can mash two or three gallons of potatoes in seconds. Sallie also used it to chop cabbage and celery to make coleslaw for her daughter's wedding. While some are fans, others mourn the loss of community—people working together—when the old ways are replaced.

Mashed Potatoes (*Gemaeschde*)

Yields about 16 gallons
Serves approximately 400 people

5 or 6 12.5-quart stainless steel buckets heaping full potatoes, peeled and cut into half-inch-thick slices

For each (12-quart) kettle of potatoes:

½ pound (2 sticks) butter
1 quart hot milk
4 tablespoons salt

Rinse peeled potatoes twice, to maintain whiteness. Fill each 12-quart kettle with potatoes. Cover with water. Bring to a boil. Cover with lid.

When the potatoes are soft, drain the water. Replace the lid, and let the potatoes steam until ready to be mashed.

Mash potatoes.

Add butter after the potatoes are mashed and there are no lumps.

Beat in the milk and salt.

Scoop the potatoes into a stainless steel container, place in a hot water bath, stir gently to maintain consistency, and keep hot until served.

Use a small saucepan to dip hot mashed potatoes into serving bowls.

Some recipes include cream cheese or sour cream in the potatoes, but many cooks don't like the "fancy" ingredients. They say that it's best to "Cook 'em soft, mash 'em well, add lots of butter, and they're good."

Gravy people

Gravy is certainly an important part of the meal, but making it does not take the sheer strength of a potato person or the lifting and carrying of a roast person. Two women are designated "gravy people," unlike the roast and potato people, who are couples.

By age seventy, Elizabeth had done pretty much every job at a wedding multiple times (except maybe hostler). So she was happy to slow down a bit. She was thinking that gravy would suit her just fine. Someone else could heave the kettles onto the stove,

"My husband doesn't know what to do with himself when he doesn't have a job with me."

and she could add the thickener, stir, adjust the burners, and stir some more. She enjoyed being in the kitchen with the others but was thinking a little about how it would be when she stayed in the wedding room for the whole service and sat down for a meal she didn't need to help make.

Kettles of celery, potatoes, and gravy are lined up on rented stoves in this wedding kitchen.
BETH OBERHOLTZER

Gravy (*Dunkes*)

Yields about 15 quarts
2 kettles serve about 350 people

Chicken broth and fat, from roasted chickens brought back by the roast
people

For one (12-quart) kettle:

2½ heaping cups flour
1 cup cornstarch
Fat, strained from the chicken broth, divided
2 tablespoons brown sugar
Salt and pepper, to taste
½ cup ginger ale

If you haven't already done so, strain the fat from the broth, reserving the
fat. Divide the chicken broth between two (12-quart) kettles. Add water
to make each kettle three-quarters full. Heat the broth.

Mix together flour and cornstarch. Mix the flour mixture with half the
reserved fat.

Pour the fat mixture into the heated broth, stirring. Bring the stock to a
boil. Continue to stir while heating.

Add the brown sugar and salt and pepper. Return to a boil, then turn off
the heat.

Add the ginger ale (this keeps the fat from separating and prevents a skin
from forming on top of the gravy). Stir. Cover with a lid.

Bring to a simmer when ready to serve.

Carry little stainless steel gravy pitchers on cake pans to prevent mishaps
when delivering to tables.

Coleslaw

Cabbage people

It requires skill and attention to be a "cabbage person" (three women are assigned). When grating fourteen or more heads of cabbage, the cabbage heads are unwieldy, and the cutting blades are sharp. After cutting each head into quarters, the workers shred the cabbage to medium fine—not mushy—on a hand grater. If leaves get out of control and come off the head? "I throw them in a box under the table and it goes out to the pigs," said Sarah.

Coleslaw served at dinner provides a cool counterpoint to its richer menu companions. The version at an Amish wedding has a sugar-and-vinegar dressing rather than the mayonnaise-heavy dressing of its creamy cousin. It also includes finely chopped celery and a garnish of chopped red sweet-and-sour peppers.

What to do with the vinegar and sugar dressing left in the mixing bowl after the coleslaw is served? Martha uses it in the garden: "That's good for the grapevines!"

Each cook station is carefully set up with the relevant recipe, ingredients, and utensils. Here the cabbage people will find everything they need to made coleslaw. JOHN HERR

Coleslaw (*Kraut*)

Yields about 6 gallons
Serves approximately 400 people

12–14 heads cabbage

For each bowl:

10 cups sugar
4 tablespoons salt
1⅓ cups apple cider vinegar
2½ quarts chopped celery (about 2 bunches)
2 cups sweet-and-sour red pepper (see next recipe)

Grate the cabbage heads and place equal amounts in two large stainless steel bowls (each bowl will hold about 12 quarts shredded cabbage).

Add the sugar, salt, and vinegar to the cabbage. Mix well. Knead cabbage until the juice runs.

Add celery and mix well.

Garnish each small serving bowl with a heaping tablespoon of sweet-and-sour red pepper.

DON SHENK

CHRISTY KAUFFMAN

Sweet-and-Sour Red Pepper

Yields 6 pint jars

1 cup white vinegar
2 cups water
3 cups sugar
10 red bell peppers, washed, cored, and diced

Mix together vinegar, water, and sugar. Bring to a boil. Pour over diced peppers.

Cold pack for 15 minutes.

Note: Cold pack is a method of canning. Fill clean glass canning jars with diced peppers. Pour the hot liquid over the peppers, leaving ½ inch headspace. Place lids on the jars and use a ring to close. Process in a boiling water canner for 15 minutes. Allow to cool, then remove from canner and allow to sit undisturbed for 12 to 24 hours.

(Canning times are subject to change according to regulations. Check your county or regional extension office.)

Recipes for the main dishes at an Amish wedding include the same basic ingredients. However, each bride's mother decides the details that are best for her daughter's celebration. Mom has cooked at other weddings and noted which dishes tasted and looked the best. She has likely studied the reference binders of her sisters and aunts. Pleasing the tastes of her own family is second nature, so she's optimistic that the wider community will enjoy the food—and not leave hungry.

Rose had a particular interest in the family garden in the summer before her wedding. Her mother planted a variety of tomatoes and agreed to turn the generous yield into their favorite barbecue sauce. It would go beautifully on the grilled chicken served at the wedding supper. CHRISTY KAUFFMAN

The bride's relatives who are assigned to cook for the wedding dinner bring their own kettles and special cooking tools from home. JOHN HERR

SIX

The Day Before a Wedding

This equipment barn has been turned into a wedding room for Elam and Mary Ann's wedding.
BETH OBERHOLTZER

Family and close friends gather at the home of the bride the morning before the wedding day. They are there for Rischding *(preparation)—doing whatever tasks they can ahead of time so their work on the wedding day goes smoothly.*

Weddings are a celebration of the bridal couple and their young friends, supported by their married elders. Aunts and uncles of the bride and her married siblings and spouses form the backbone of the operation. Grandparents have taken a step back from the heavy work, but the *Mammis* (grandmothers) may cut fruit and wash dishes while the *Daadis* (grandfathers) chop celery. Key assignments have been given, and most workers know their responsibilities.

Though many of the bride's relatives are working on the day of the wedding, her father and mother, having planned all to the smallest detail, will be off the clock on the day itself. They must give final guidance to their deputies the day before, then step aside and trust that all will go as intended.

"Don't forget to make a big pot of coffee early for the work people."

Paper ladies have received instructions from the bride's mother, including who is assigned to what jobs under their management. They meet with the mom and make sure they know where everything is for cooking and serving the meals. The paper ladies and the cooks set up each cooking station with equipment and recipes and make sure all the food is marked. They may also be given a list of church ladies who don't have other assignments who can be called on if needed.

When Katherine goes to help the day before a wedding, she always takes her own twelve-quart kettle, a few good knives, a utility tub, and a roast pan or two.

The roast, celery, potato, and cabbage people make stuffing, chop celery, prep celery for centerpieces, scrub potatoes, and grate cabbage. Desserts for supper are underway. Workers cut up fruit for the salad, ready to be mixed up the next morning.

Chest ladies assign and mark serving dishes for all the menu items and follow the direction of paper ladies regarding which dishes go with each stove. They fill dozens of salt and pepper shakers and set up sugar bowls and creamers.

While the paper ladies and cooks swarm the wedding kitchen, the Eck tenders set up their workplace. It is a dedicated room or area close to the wedding kitchen and near a door leading into the wedding room where the bride and groom will be seated. Here they will prepare special foods and showcase treats and food gifts from guests. There is a kitchen section with its own appliances; if the bride's parents have purchased a new refrigerator and stove for the couple, they can be used here beforehand.

Kettles of celery, crates of potatoes, and stacks of dishes await the cooks and dish ladies on the morning of the wedding. **LEFT:** CHRISTY KAUFFMAN, **RIGHT:** JOHN HERR

This is not the usual setup in the rec room within Omar's horse barn. He enjoyed seeing the decorated table where the Eck tenders at his daughter's wedding collected and displayed food gifts. The Eck tenders prepared delicacies for the bride and groom in a small adjacent Eck kitchen. JOHN HERR

The day before the wedding, the Eck tenders decorate the Eck table display and organize the ingredients for the unique bridal party menu items. They may create parfaits in goblets by layering yogurt or gelatin with fruit and whipped cream and chill them overnight. They may cook eggs for deviled eggs or cut up tropical fruit for a salad. The fancy table settings and serving dishes are double-checked and stacked at the ready.

The women Eck tenders enjoy being creative with decorations. Butter sculptures are popular. Leah and her fellow tenders created two pillar candles out of two pounds of butter each, then rolled them in sugar and cinnamon and pushed little battery-operated tea lights into the tops. Bridal couples have also enjoyed butter molded into sculptures that say "Love" or "Mr. & Mrs." or are shaped into flowers or leaves.

The Forgeher receive detailed instructions from the bridal couple and bride's parents on seating guests for both the church service and meals, as well as the overall schedule of the wedding day. Along with setting up benches, they make sure the council room—where the members of the ministry will meet with the bride and groom during the service—has benches for the ministers and chairs for the couple. They also lend a hand in setting up other gathering places.

All available men pitch in to carry benches from the two or three bench wagons and arrange them in the wedding room following a predetermined layout. Men and women will be seated separately, in order of age and relationship to the bridal couple. Two or three rows of chairs are set up at the center for the bride and groom, side sitters, ministers, and close relatives. Copies of the *Ausbund* are placed at intervals on the benches. The layout echoes how a room is arranged for a regular church service, but for more than twice the number of attendees.

The bride's uncles, several of whom will likely be on duty as Forgeher, will be responsible for creating tables for the wedding dinner from the benches used in the service. They practice setting up the dining tables the day before the wedding and make note of the bench numbering and mark the floor with tape so they can position tables precisely when it's transition time.

When Samuel and Laura's daughter got married, the wedding took place in their equipment barn. Samuel temporarily nailed two rows of two-by-fours to the walls of the wedding room with screws placed at regular intervals where male guests could hang their hats. Since the black hats

When evening falls, one of the guests is assigned to turn on the battery-powered lamps in the wedding room. He also stays alert in case batteries need to be switched out. A cord leads from the battery charging station to a gasoline-powered generator. Many farms also gather energy from solar panels on barn and house roofs. CHRISTY KAUFFMAN

The layout of benches and chairs for a wedding follows the same pattern—whether it takes place in a wedding house, a barn, or a house. The bridal couple and ministers sit in the center with guests behind and at right angles to them, men on one side, women on the other.
TOP: CHRISTY KAUFFMAN, **BOTTOM:** JOHN HERR

Omar and Lydia had a temporary addition built to their barn to house the wedding kitchen when their daughter got married in November. JOHN HERR

look virtually the same, the wearer must make a mental note of where he left his. The spots are sometimes numbered, which is a help, and owner's names are written inside the hats.

Though the Eck display and gift areas are decorated, there is virtually no decoration in the wedding room, whether it is set up for the church service or for the meals and singing that take place later. The focus is on the significance of the occasion and not external ornamentation.

Cleaning has already been completed, but several women take a final sweep through the house. They look for crumbs, spots, and smudges and anything out of place. Each gathering place is reviewed to be sure it's ready.

When guests arrive at a wedding, they are directed, sometimes with signs, to areas where their fellows congregate.

- Married women gather in the wedding room.

- Married men meet in the forebay or in a space in the barn.

- Young women and girls assemble in the living room, recreation room, or the post-dinner singing area.

During the morning before the wedding, "boys" ranging in age from teens through young men in their twenties will gather in a cleared section of the horse barn. It's set up for them to relax or play games. Depending on the weather, both boys and girls may socialize here in the afternoon. JOHN HERR

The day before Rose's wedding, her brother and niece rake a load of stone smooth on the driveway. CHRISTY KAUFFMAN

- Young men and boys converge in a cleaned-out section of the barn or a shop or garage.

- Mothers with babies are shown the "baby room" (which may also serve as the council room) in case the little ones get fussy or need to nap.

An area is also set up in a recreation room or finished basement where gifts are collected and where the bridal couple goes immediately after dinner to open gifts and enjoy listening to their friends sing.

Younger siblings are often assigned the last-minute outdoor cleanup. They rake the yard and the gravel driveway, sweep the porches, give the house windows a final polish, and are on call for other chores as needed. Susan's little sister even picked up stray leaves one at a time to make sure the yard looked its best.

Parents and grandparents will be seated in chairs at the front when the bride and groom open their gifts right after dinner. Dozens of youth stand around and behind them and sing gospel songs selected by the bridal couple for the hour or so that the gift-opening takes. JOHN HERR

After the wedding house was set up adjacent to the house, Rose's father and brothers built a covered passage between the wedding kitchen on the lower level of the house and the stand-alone wedding house for her October wedding. CHRISTY KAUFFMAN

The men make sure wagons and feeders are set up for the horses, stalls readied, and tents erected. Water containers are checked and hoses dragged into place.

The day before his daughter's wedding, Samuel moved the hay out of his barn to his brother's barn across the road to allow space for wagons around which to tie horses in his barn. The morning of the wedding, he moved his dozen draft horses from their stalls to the field so his guests' horses could be in the stalls.

There can easily be fifty or more people working the day before the wedding, and they eat a hearty brunch together. It usually includes over a dozen breakfast casseroles brought by family or neighbors. There is also fruit salad, yogurt, and shoofly pie, plus orange juice, coffee, and hot chocolate.

Having arrived at seven in the morning, most workers are ready to head home by early afternoon. The bride and groom have been working alongside family and friends all day. They and their side sitters already washed the celery. Next they'll rake and use the leaf blower to make sure everything is tidy. In the evening, the couple may have a bit of a breather and can relax with the bride's family before the business of tomorrow. Maybe the neighbors will bring supper.

All is ready the day before Abram and Susan's wedding. The benches have been removed from the bench wagons and set up in the wedding room (not pictured). On the wedding day, the guests' horses will be tied to the hay wagons under the rented tent. JOHN HERR

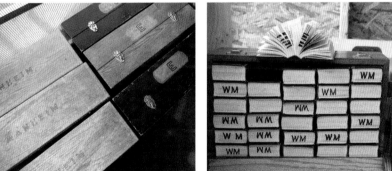

Three or four bench wagons, each containing boxes of the Ausbund *and* Gesangbuch *in addition to benches and chairs, are needed for one wedding. Here, the "WM" (West Manheim) written on the edges ensures that the hymnbooks will get back to their home.*
CHRISTY KAUFFMAN

SEVEN

The Wedding Day: Morning

Guests arrive at Benuel and Barbara's wedding on a beautiful morning in early December. JOHN HERR

Everyone in the hosting household is up bright and early on the day of the wedding. There's a push to complete chores and eat breakfast by the time the first workers—Forgeher, side sitters, and hostlers— begin arriving as early as six thirty in the morning.

An Amish wedding is an all-day event. Most follow the same general schedule, though times may vary a bit according to family's preferences. The bride and groom are active participants from when they begin greeting guests before seven in the morning to when they bid farewell from their seats at the Eck in the late evening.

Arrival and preparation

The mother of the bride has put in long hours and planned carefully for this day; her helpers have been told what needs to be done and when. They now shield her from tasks so she can concentrate on the guests. It is up to her to set the tone for the day. As Sarah noted, the mom needs "to be gracious and calm; she shouldn't get fired up."

The bride's mother's number one guest is the groom's mother, whom she attends throughout the day. The bride's father similarly accompanies the

Wedding Day Schedule

Arrival and preparation

6:30   Helpers arrive and get to work
         Bridal couple and attendants greet guests

Church service

7:30   Guests are ushered to their seats

8:00   Service begins

8:30   Hostlers and other workers have a snack in wedding kitchen

10:30   Wedding ceremony within service

Dinner and afternoon

11:30   Wedding room transition to dining room

12:00   First meal seating served, two others follow

12:30   Singing and opening gifts in designated area

2:00   Visiting time and youth games

3:00   Afternoon singing in wedding room; snacks served
         at afternoon table

4:00   Farewell to some guests

Supper and evening

5:00   Multiple shifts eat at Family Table

6:00   First serving at Big Table

7:00   Bridal couple and young people served at Big Table

8:00   Evening singing in wedding room
         Guests begin leaving and give well-wishes to newlyweds

9:30   Evening singing ends, most guests are gone

groom's father. Other members of the bride's extended family are on work duty.

Hostlers are the first to show up. The father of the bride, sometimes via the Forgeher, gives direction regarding buggy parking and where to house the horses. Hostlers must also keep the barnyard and other common areas clear of horse manure. They are often called chore boys since they may have jobs beyond tending the horses. If specific chores must be done in the evening, they are given instructions for that.

Guests generally arrive between seven and seven thirty in the morning, which means the hostlers must step lively. They direct the parking, help unhitch horses, lead the horses to water, and then settle them in their stalls or at feeders. When it is particularly busy, a hostler may lead two or three horses at the same time. Owners generally try to keep an eye out as to where their horses are tied so they can check on them later.

"We stack 'em in as they come. If they're packed in the stall they can't kick as easy."

Paper ladies make sure they arrive in plenty of time to communicate any yet-to-be-assigned jobs. Papers in hand that list helpers' names and assignments, they join other women in the wedding room, where married women gather to socialize before the wedding. If women who are

Guests park their buggies around the barn when they arrive as the hostlers direct. JOHN HERR

Nearby guests walk to the wedding whereas those who live farther away drive their horses and buggies. It is also common for guests to hire English drivers to transport them in cars or vans when distance makes it necessary. JOHN HERR

connected to the bride don't already know their jobs, they present themselves to the two women who are "holding the papers." The workers, mostly aunts and older married sisters, convey assignments to their husbands, who are likely gathered in the barn with the other married men.

"Are you the paper lady? What's my job?"

The cooks head immediately to their stations in the wedding kitchen and consult their recipes. They need to time their dishes to allow for a pause while they attend part of the service in the wedding room; they will then return to the kitchen to finish the cooking and have the food ready to dish up at noon. The paper ladies work in the kitchen with the cooks during the church service.

Though there may be carefully handcrafted signs pointing to the different gathering places, Forgeher are on hand to organize guests and direct when needed: two couples are on duty inside the wedding room, two

After guests at a November wedding park their buggies (above), hostlers lead the horses under the tent and tie them to farm wagons stacked with hay. Signs outside (right) direct where guests should gather in the morning before a January wedding. "Clothes" indicates where the women's shawls can be hung.
ABOVE: CHRISTY KAUFFMAN, **RIGHT:** BETH OBERHOLTZER

couples are outside. They keep special watch for English guests who may need guidance. The Forgeher men review the wedding room to make sure the chairs are set up correctly for the bridal party and ministers and that benches are neatly aligned and hymnals in place.

The Eck tender couples begin setting up their display and preparing the ingredients for tasty additions to the dinner menu—perhaps steak on the grill or shrimp cocktail. Bridal treats often include bouquets of strawberries dipped in chocolate, fruit kabobs, and dessert parfaits.

The Eck tenders also receive food gifts for the couple, make note of givers' names, and arrange the gifts at the Eck display. Eck gifts are presented on plates or in containers (fancy dishes or platters or plastic storage containers) that are part of the gift. Gifts brought by family generally include several cakes, dishes of candy, platters of ham and cheese or vegetables. Perhaps there are also fancy fruits, custom sweets, and bologna rolled up with cream cheese or arranged into flower shapes. The Eck display often incorporates lovely glassware, decoratively lettered Bible verses, and occasionally, vases of flowers. Cakes on stands are arrayed on the top level of the table.

A generation ago, a dozen cakes might be brought as Eck gifts. Samuel explained that when he got married nearly thirty years ago, it was said that "however many cakes you get, that's how many children you will have." He didn't keep track of the cakes, "but I do know how many children I have."

Since there has been a recent increase in guests bringing gifts with them to the wedding rather than giving them to the couple at later visits, gift attendant is a relatively new assignment. This role may be filled by one or more of the bride's buddy girls, sisters, or nieces. They display the gifts on a table for the couple to open after dinner.

The grid on the walls of this wedding room is formed by the barn's wooden frame within the aluminum siding. The chandelier decorated with greens in the far right corner of the room hangs above where the Eck will be when the dinner tables are set up. The men who transform the benches into tables are guided by the numbers stenciled on the benches. JOHN HERR

Arriving guests shake hands all around within their peer groups and with others as they pass by, chatting briefly. They may take a few minutes to view the Eck table and gift display.

Before seven in the morning, the bridal couple and their side sitters are settled in their chairs inside the wedding room near the door. Upon arrival, most family members and youth group friends greet the couple; women congregated in the wedding room shake hands with them and are welcomed.

Church service and wedding ceremony

An Amish wedding service in Lancaster County is quite similar to a customary Amish church service, but with hymns, scripture readings, and sermons that focus on the theme of marriage. The German-language hymns sung in unison at the beginning and end of the service are from the *Ausbund* and are matched with a variety of traditional tunes. Scripture and prayers are read or recited in High German, and the sermons and testimonials are in High German intertwined with Pennsylvania German.

Male guests are directed by male Forgeher, and female guests are directed by female Forgeher. At seven thirty, when it's time to prepare for the wedding service, Forgeher collect the men and boys from the barn and outbuildings and the girls from their visiting area. Lists are posted, and the Forgeher carry copies, of young men and young women's names noting in what order they should be seated.

Ministers and close family members enter the wedding room, shake hands with the couple, and are directed to their chairs. First seated on one side of the room are the bride's and groom's fathers and grandfathers. Ministers are seated next in the center. The bride's and groom's mothers and grandmothers are seated on the other side of the room.

The remainder of the men and boys enter the wedding room through a door at one side and are directed to their places on the men's side. At the same time, women and girls come in from the other direction and are seated on the opposite side of the room. The order and where each person sits are determined by age, marital status, and their relationship to

Seating for the Church Service / Wedding Ceremony

Presiding bishop

Bride's and groom's grandmothers	Bride's mother	Three ministers who have a part in the service (facing one another)	Bride's father	Bride's and groom's grandfathers
Groom's married women cousins	Groom's mother		Groom's father	Groom's married men cousins
Groom's married women neighbors	Groom's married sisters and sisters-in-law	Bride and her side sitters on one side	Groom's married brothers and brothers-in-law	Groom's married men neighbors
Groom's married women church people	Groom's aunts	Groom and his side sitters on other side	Groom's uncles	Groom's married men church people
Ministers' wives	Groom's boss's wife	Four to eight other bishops, ministers, and deacons (facing one another)	Groom's boss	

The bride and groom, their side sitters, and the ministry sit in the center row of chairs. (The presiding bishop sits perpendicular to this center row.) Guests are seated beginning in the second row, men on one side and women on the other, in descending order of relative importance and marital status. The bride's married aunts and sisters are working in the kitchen, so when they attend for just the wedding part of the service, they sit on benches at the back.

Young unmarried folks fill the benches behind the married folks and on the benches that are at right angles to the others. They, too, are divided by gender, relationship to the bride and groom, and age. Unmarried siblings are seated first, followed by close friends, couples who were just married or just published, cousins, and friends. The specifics are unique to each bride and groom.

Non-Amish guests sit at right angles to the rows of chairs, facing the bishop.

the bridal couple; it is fine-tuned based on the makeup of the bridal couple's families.

Since the bride's family is hosting the wedding, the groom's family are "special people," the honored guests. The congregation at this point is largely related to the groom since the bride's married relatives and friends are preparing the food and performing a variety of other tasks. But space is reserved near the back for them to take their seats when their work allows it.

Younger folks are seated, men with the men and women with the women, in roughly the same order as the older folks: unmarried brothers and sisters, couples who were just married or just published, cousins, and friends. English (non-Amish) guests sit on chairs at the back.

The bridal couple remains sitting at the outer edge while the wedding room fills with guests. When everyone is seated, an uncle or married brother of the groom leads out to begin the first song, page 378 in the *Ausbund*, which describes the church as Christ's bride. The church getting ready for Christ's return is likened to a bride getting ready to meet her bridegroom (Matthew 25:1–10, Revelation 21:2). When the first two lines are completed, the ministers (bishops, ministers, deacons) who are present leave the wedding room and go to the council room, followed by the

LEFT: *Books at hand for the ministers, both in German:* Gebet *(Prayer) book and* Neue Testament *(New Testament).* **RIGHT:** *The hymn sung from the* Ausbund *at the end of the service is "Gelobt sei Gott" ("Praise God in the Highest").* CHRISTY KAUFFMAN

bride and groom. The side sitters also leave the room, perhaps to get a snack, then return when the bride and groom do.

There can easily be a dozen members of the ministry at a wedding. This includes the bishop, ministers, and deacon from the bride's church; grandfathers, uncles, brothers, or friends of the bride and groom who have been ordained; the bishop from the groom's church; and if the bride has been a teacher, any students' fathers who have been ordained.

The bishop who will marry the couple may be from the groom's district, a relative or friend of the groom or bride, or invited separately. If the ministry attending from the churches or within the family doesn't yield two bishops, the family invites another bishop to ensure that the wedding can take place if one bishop is somehow indisposed. Stories are told of dramatic efforts to secure a bishop when a service was set to begin and there was no bishop in attendance.

If the wedding is held on the first floor of the home, the council room might be an upstairs bedroom; if the wedding takes place in the barn or a separate wedding house, the council room is a nearby prepared space. As the congregation continues singing, the bride and groom meet with all the ministers for their one and only marital counseling session.

The couple sits beside each other and faces the semicircle of ministers. The senior minister of the bride's district leads the council. He and others offer words of encouragement and advice. One of the bishops asks once more whether the couple has remained pure, and they answer in the affirmative. It is a final check for whether all is in order.

The counseling conversation likely takes about twenty or thirty minutes, during which the congregation continues singing. The bride and groom join their side sitters back in the wedding room and take their places in a row of chairs at the center of the wedding room. The bride and groom sit facing each other, their side sitters beside them.

The ministers stay another ten or fifteen minutes to plan the service. They decide now which bishop will take the lead (if more than one is present)—giving the main sermon and marrying the couple—and who will play a supporting role. The selection of marrying bishop depends on how long ago a bishop was ordained and how close each bishop is to the bride.

The bridal couple does not decide which bishop will perform the wedding ceremony, nor do they invite someone for that specific reason. It is decided by the ministry, though sometimes with a bit of a hint by way of the bride's father.

By the time the couple has seated themselves in the wedding room, the congregation has moved on to page 770 of the *Ausbund* for "Das Loblied," a sacred hymn of praise sung at all Amish church services. By the end of this song, the ministers have returned to the wedding room and taken their places beside the bridal couple on the center chairs.

The first sermon, given by a minister who is often a relative of the groom, lasts up to a half hour. It draws on the Old Testament for advice related to marriage, beginning with creation and mentioning the importance of Eve as a companion to Adam: "And the LORD God said, It is not good that the man should be alone; I will make him an help meet for him" (Genesis 2:18). This sermon wraps up with mention of Noah and his sons—who each had one wife—and their righteous lives.

The congregation turns toward the benches and kneels in silent prayer. Then they stand, still facing the benches, for a reading from Matthew on Jesus' teachings about divorce, including, "Wherefore they are no more twain, but one flesh. What therefore God hath joined together, let not man put asunder" (Matthew 19:6).

A Cup of Cold Water

Toward the beginning of the presiding bishop's sermon, one of the Forgeher hands him a glass of water; the bishop takes a drink and puts the glass down. He will take occasional sips throughout the service. Presenting the glass is a somewhat ceremonial gesture that represents hospitality as a Christian virtue. Mother of the bride Sarah was touched when she noticed that her brother picked one of her most beautiful crystal glasses to fill and give to the bishop. "He really put his heart into that choice," she said.

The presiding bishop delivers the main sermon. He references stories in the Old Testament, then moves on to read and explain passages in the New Testament that support marriage as a positive experience, offer advice for a successful marriage, explain each person's role in the marriage, and cite community support of marriage.

In the sermon, the bishop draws extensively on 1 Corinthians 7, 1 Peter 3, Ephesians 5, and Ruth 1.

- "Husbands, love your wives, even as Christ also loved the church, and gave himself for it . . ." (Ephesians 5:25).

- "For this cause shall a man leave his father and mother, and shall be joined unto his wife, and they two shall be one flesh" (Ephesians 5:31).

- "The wife is bound by the law as long as her husband liveth; but if her husband be dead, she is at liberty to be married to whom she will; only in the Lord" (1 Corinthians 7:39).

- "And Ruth said, Intreat me not to leave thee, or to return from following after thee: for whither thou goest, I will go; and where thou lodgest, I will lodge: thy people shall be my people, and thy God my God" (Ruth 1:16).

Careful instruction is given to the couple on the importance of maintaining a godly home, being faithful church members, and helping others who are in need.

The bishop turns to the book of Tobit in the Apocrypha and relates the story of the pious Tobit and his relative Sarah, who suffer afflictions. Upon praying to God for deliverance, God sends the angel Raphael to act as intercessor. Sarah marries Tobit's son Tobias, and their faith is rewarded.

"We paper ladies sit way in the back so we can slip out quietly and take care of the eats."

At the end of the sermon, the bishop speaks to those gathered. (The singing and scripture reading during the service are in High German; the sermons are in a mix of High German and Pennsylvania German. The wording here has been translated into English and is a close approximation of what is generally said.) "Here

Careful Timing

Working out the timing for a wedding can require finesse when one is both a seated guest at a wedding and a cook preparing food to be eaten immediately after the service. Fortunately, an Amish wedding service follows an established format; guests know just what to expect and when. The service begins at eight o'clock with two hymns followed by a series of sermons and testimonies.

Hostlers are on work duty during the service. After settling all the horses in their temporary quarters, the hostlers are given a snack in the kitchen with the other workers, then take their places in the wedding room near the wall, close to the front, at about nine thirty. Eck tenders typically join the worshipers after the service has begun and leave to return to their tasks right after the couple is married.

The Forgeher are generally seated throughout the service, though several remain alert to guide English guests to their seats.

At roughly half past ten, the bride and groom are invited to step forward. Prior to that, depending on the status of their dishes-in-progress, the paper ladies and cooks slide onto their benches toward the back of the wedding room. They've cleaned up the kitchen and adjusted stove and oven temperatures so they can listen to the bishop's message and attend the marriage ceremony. Toward the end of the service, before the final sermon and testimonies, the cooks return to the kitchen to put the final touches on their dishes while the hostlers head out to feed and water the horses.

are two who have requested to be joined in marriage," says the bishop. "The brother is (*groom's name*) and the sister is (*bride's name*). If there is a scriptural reason that this should not occur, now is the time to make it known. After this formality any complaint will not be accepted." The bishop pauses deliberately and takes a sip of water. "Now is a good time to say a prayer for the couple."

The bishop invites the couple to come forward to take their vows while the side sitters remain seated. "There is no one here who will withhold this doing," he says. "If your intent is still the same as it was this morning, you can come forth in the name of the Lord." The bride and groom rise, join hands, and stand before him. They are led through a series of questions and affirm their belief in the scriptural order for man and woman to be one, recognize the Lord's direction in their choice of spouse, and acknowledge the power of prayer. They promise to support each other and stand as Christian husband and wife, vowing to remain together with love, compassion, and patience for one another.

The bishop joins their hands together and says, "The God of Abraham, and the God of Isaac, and the God of Jacob be with you and help you together and give his blessings richly unto you, and to this I wish you God's blessings to a good beginning and maintained to a blessed end. And this in and through Jesus Christ. Amen."

"Go forth in the name of the Lord as a husband and wife," the bishop says, and the couple returns to their chairs. It is a solemn time, the seriousness respected by the couple and congregation. There is no outward indication of the joy of the occasion, though there may be tears.

The bishop wraps up his sermon, continuing with the marriage theme and sometimes recounting the remainder of the Tobit chronicle. After concluding, he calls on the other bishops in attendance if they are led to comment ("give testimony") on the message, add their own thoughts, or wish God's blessing on the couple. The bride's father, groom's father, and grandfathers are invited to speak if they wish.

Several of the attending bishops may each offer two to five minutes of testimony from their seats. Fathers or grandfathers may have remarks.

The presiding bishop has closing comments. The congregation turns toward their seats and kneels as he reads a final prayer from the *Christenpflicht* prayer book and recites the Lord's Prayer.

The congregation stands, still facing their seats, to hear the final scripture reading from 2 Corinthians. This passage is recited at the end of all Amish church services, including funerals and weddings.

"Finally, brethren, farewell. Be perfect, be of good comfort, be of one mind, live in peace; and the God of love and peace shall be with you. Greet one another with an holy kiss. All the saints salute you. The grace of the Lord Jesus Christ, and the love of God, and the communion of the Holy Ghost, be with you all. Amen" (2 Corinthians 13:11–14).

All congregants bend a knee at the closing "amen," then turn and sit to sing the final hymn, the first four verses of page 712 in the *Ausbund*, "Gelobt sei Gott" ("Praise God in the Highest").

It is common at events that draw a large number of people—such as weddings—for drivers to remove the bridles and tie their horses to hay wagons, then park the buggies elsewhere. JOHN HERR

EIGHT

The Wedding Day:
Afternoon and Evening

Cooks have been working all morning to make sure dinner will be ready at noon shortly after the wedding service ends. BETH OBERHOLTZER

With the last note of the final hymn still hanging in the air, the energy in the wedding room changes. There is no dramatic recessional; the bride and groom and their side sitters leave in a leisurely fashion. The young people head out at the same time followed by the hundreds of other guests. Within ten minutes, most guests have left the wedding room, and the assigned men, many of them the bride's uncles, begin the bench-to-table conversion.

Upon exiting the wedding room, the newlyweds go to the bride's bedroom, where, if she's wearing a black covering, she changes to a white one. The groom may—as custom calls for—go outside and shake hands with the assembled men. Or the couple simply spends a few quiet minutes together until they're summoned to eat.

Time to eat

Twenty minutes after the service has ended, the benches have been transformed into a series of tables. Each table is created from three benches and added trusses that raise them to table height and lock them together. The assigned men know what group of benches they are responsible for and address them

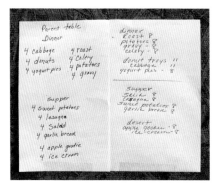

Instructions are taped to the wedding room wall for the table waiters. The list includes how many serving dishes of each menu item should be provided to each table for each meal. The Family (or Parent) Table list is on the left; the Big Table list is on the right. Cooks work quickly to keep up with the several seatings of guests at each table. **LEFT:** JOHN HERR, **RIGHT:** BETH OBERHOLTZER

immediately. Following a carefully annotated drawing, the men arrange the tables to create a huge U-shaped Big Table that seats around a hundred guests and a long Family Table that seats roughly fifty guests. They then place benches on both sides of each table. Two people can fit on a three-foot bench; thus diners are allotted about eighteen inches of space.

A separate table (Small Table) is often set up toward the outer edge of the room to serve English guests, schoolchildren invited because their teacher is the bride, or relatives who are "in the *bann*" (being shunned).[7] Additional tables to serve an assortment of workers, family, and guests are likely set up in the kitchen trailer, if one is attached to the wedding house, and in the wedding kitchen itself.

Though family members who are shunned don't eat with the others, they are routinely invited to weddings and—if aunts, uncles, or married siblings of the bride—take on their traditional tasks. Rather than sitting down to eat, they may simply snack in the wedding kitchen.

While tables are being assembled, the chest (dish) ladies direct their husbands to move the chests into the wedding room to prepare to set the tables. Almost before the tables are positioned, cloth tablecloths are whipped into place; dishes, flatware, and glasses are placed at each setting;

During meals and singing, Rose and her groom will sit on chairs that she decorated with lace. CHRISTY KAUFFMAN

napkins are laid down; and water is poured. At regular intervals on each table, the waiters place butter and jelly, small bowls of coleslaw, heaping trays of cookies and doughnuts, and maybe fruit salad.

Outside the meeting-room-turned-dining-room, guests begin arranging themselves in the appropriate order to enter the room—essentially the same order in which they were seated for the church service. The Forgeher check their notes and began seating people—touching an arm here and a shoulder there to direct each to their assigned spot. The Family Table fills quickly, followed by the Big Table. Just thirty minutes after the service ended, the room has been transformed to a dining room with more than 150 guests seated and ready to be served.

The groom and bride (at his left) are seated at the Eck—or corner—of the Big Table with their side sitters. Young single women are arrayed on the bride's side, young single men on the groom's side. This includes siblings and nieces and nephews of the couple who are age nine and older. When the Forgeher sees that everyone is in place at the Big Table and

First Seating for Dinner

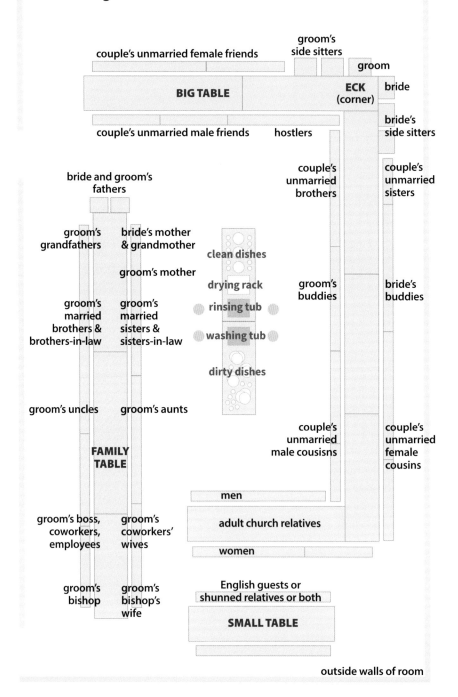

couple's unmarried female friends

groom's side sitters

groom

BIG TABLE

ECK (corner)

bride

couple's unmarried male friends   hostlers

bride's side sitters

bride and groom's fathers

couple's unmarried brothers

couple's unmarried sisters

groom's grandfathers

bride's mother & grandmother

clean dishes

groom's mother

drying rack

groom's buddies

bride's buddies

groom's married brothers & brothers-in-law

groom's married sisters & sisters-in-law

rinsing tub

washing tub

dirty dishes

groom's uncles   groom's aunts

FAMILY TABLE

couple's unmarried male cousisns

couple's unmarried female cousins

men

groom's boss, coworkers, employees

groom's coworkers' wives

adult church relatives

women

groom's bishop

groom's bishop's wife

English guests or shunned relatives or both

SMALL TABLE

outside walls of room

Wedding Room Turned Dining Room

TABLE LAYOUT

Though the specific layout of the tables varies depending on the dimensions of the wedding room and the location of doors leading in and out, there is always a Big Table set up in a U-shape, a Family Table, and a Small Table. Additional tables may be set up in the wedding room, wedding kitchen, or recreation room.

Whether in home, barn, shop, or wedding house, tables are arranged to allow guests to be seated quickly and efficiently and to allow easy access from the kitchens for table waiters and Eck tenders. Dishwashing stations are set up wherever there's space.

Tables are set at least two and often three times to get everyone fed.

DINNER SEATINGS

Most guests at the Family Table are the groom's relatives since the bride's family is working.

First seating: Bride and groom (seated at the Eck) and their side sitters; buddies, close friends, unmarried siblings; hostlers; close relatives of the groom; bride's parents and grandparents, groom's married siblings.

Second seating: Eck tenders (seated at the Eck); distant relatives, remaining young people; bishops and ministers and their wives; relatives who are church people.

Third seating: Forgeher and paper ladies; bride's aunts, uncles, and married siblings who were working; cooks including roast and potato people; remaining church people and neighbors; schoolchildren if the bride has been a teacher.

AFTERNOON

- Guests gather in the wedding room to socialize.
- Young people sit at the Big Table for the afternoon singing. Older folks sit on rows of chairs and benches in the center of the room (i.e., in place of the dishwashing station pictured in the diagram).

SUPPER SEATINGS

Some guests leave before supper; however, hundreds are still present.

Three or four seatings at the Family Table: Couples who will be table waiters for the two seatings at the Big Table; Eck table waiters who aren't immediate family; church people; neighbors.

First seating at the Big Table: Bride's parents seated at the Eck; parents of groom; groom's married siblings and close relatives; bride's siblings' parents-in-law; parents' buddy group couples.

Second seating at the Big Table: Bride and groom seated at the Eck, unmarried young people seated as pairs.

EVENING

- Young people sit at tables for the evening singing in the same pairs as at supper. Older married folks sit in the center on rows of chairs and benches.

◀ *Unlike what's shown in the diagram, the bride's parents may be seated at the head of the Family Table with the groom's parents facing each other across the table. The groom's married siblings would be next, then grandparents—men on one side, women on the other.*

ready to eat, he tells the groom, "Everybody's seated. Go ahead." Or he simply nods across the room. The groom bows his head for the traditional silent prayer prior to eating. Everyone immediately quiets and also bows their heads. After a moment of silence, those sitting nearby raise their heads when they see the groom raise his at the end of the prayer. The motion quickly moves around the table. A silent prayer is offered at the beginning and end of each seating at each table.

As soon as heads are raised from the predinner silent prayer, the parade of food begins. Cooks fill dozens of serving bowls and hand them off to the table waiters, who then pass them, family style, to the waiting guests.

The just-married couple and their side sitters are waited on by the Eck tenders, ready to cater to their every whim. The bride and groom and their side sitters eat from fine china and sip their drinks from fancy goblets; their guests eat from melamine plates and drink water from shatterproof tumblers.

Along with the traditional fare that is served to all, the newlyweds—and their side sitters—are offered a variety of special tidbits presented on little supper plates. There may be deviled eggs, shrimp, or pieces of lobster drenched in butter. Brown butter is available for their mashed potatoes. Sprigs of parsley may decorate the roast, which is perhaps topped with a lovely slice of chicken or turkey breast. Dessert is often supplemented with strawberries dipped in chocolate, decorative candies, and precious little cakes. There is much more food offered than can comfortably be eaten. But it is a rare chance for the young couple to be indulged—maybe a few bites of this, a few bites of that. Whatever catches one's fancy. And they may ask that some of the treats be shared with family and close friends as well.

The Eck tenders carry some of the gift foods from the Eck display outside of the wedding room into the now-dining room. A butter sculpture may now grace the Eck table in front of the newlyweds, along with fruit bouquets, trays of cookies, and other delectables.

Since wedding services and meals take place in a "church," the area is to be kept free of decoration. Traditionally, any embellishments on the dinner tables and at the Eck where the couple sits consist of a variety of foods displayed on attractive dishes. Bowls spaced out on the tables for all guests hold coleslaw and fruit, while platters or tiered stands display individual desserts. A modern bride may top the tables with lace runners and branches of eucalyptus or evergreens. A step further might be a few sprays of baby's breath, a row of pumpkins, or stalks of wheat. Though older folks may be disconcerted, small changes are gradually accepted.

Seatings at the two main tables—the Family Table and the Big Table—occur independent of each other. Each has a Forgeher team and specific table waiters to tend them. As soon as all are seated, those at the Family Table (where close family members eat at the first seating) offer a silent prayer of thanks and are served their meal, usually before the Big Table is filled. Since there are many waiting to eat, there is no time to dawdle; two shifts may eat at the Family Table at the same time one shift eats at the substantially larger Big Table.

The first dinner seating at the Big Table lasts about thirty minutes. It allows the bridal couple time to enjoy the main meal and their special eats. They may hand dishes of candy down the table to share with others.

After eating, people on each side of the table collect their dirty dishes and add them to the growing stack being passed down the row to the end of the table. Uncles and church men who are on dishwashing duty patrol the room and carry dirty dishes to the washing station. As quickly as the dishes are washed, they're rinsed and dried and set on the tables again.

The Forgeher for each table has been keeping an eye on the clock and the status of the food service. When he sees that people are done eating, he tells the head of the table that "everybody's finished." The bride's father at the Family Table or the groom at the Big Table bows his head and commences the silent prayer that ends the meal. All quickly quiet their conversations and put their heads down. Senior men at each table lead prayers at subsequent seatings.

"It's a real chicken house with everybody talking and laughing."

More than 150 diners talking and laughing and thirty workers serving and washing dishes can cause quite a din. After a "shh!" travels around the room, there is dead silence while one of the tables offers a silent prayer to begin or end a meal. Then the merriment starts up again.

At the end of a closing prayer, the diners from the first seating promptly file out of the room, allowing the Forgeher to usher in the guests for the second seating. The Eck tenders take the place of the bride and groom to eat at the Eck while the ministers and remaining relatives and young people fill out the rest of the Big Table.

Unlike the leisurely thirty minutes that is commonly taken for the first-seating guests to eat at the Big Table, people at the second seating generally take about twenty minutes to eat.

The third seating, which also takes about fifteen or twenty minutes, is the time for workers, church people, and neighbors to have their meal. The uncles who have been madly washing dishes can now have a bite to eat before washing the final dinner dishes.

Family and guests are steeped in the understanding of their status related to others in each situation or mix of people. On the wedding day, the groom's family and bride's parents are honored while the rest of the bride's family—particularly married aunts and uncles, siblings, and in-laws—does the work. Age and marital status inform both where people are seated and the jobs they are assigned.

The details of seating at each wedding vary a bit depending on the makeup of the couple's families, but the pattern is familiar to all guests. Church people and neighbors gather to celebrate, but they do not expect to eat at the first seating and maybe not the second. They are in a supporting role this time around, though it will change when they attend the wedding of a young person who is a close relative of theirs.

Practical generosity

In keeping with the Amish's modest lifestyle, wedding gifts to an Amish couple are practical. There is no gift registry, since the community already has a good idea of what the couple needs. It is common for a man who is part of a married couple to give a gift to the groom, such as tools or outdoor maintenance gear, and for the woman to give a gift to the bride, often dishware, canned food, or household items. A bride's buddy girls may all chip in to buy a gift together.

Jay and Rose's nieces and nephews gave them toys carefully wrapped and collected in a red wagon. One young niece drew a picture of family members on the brown wrapper (top). Samuel made a drying rack for a neighbor's daughter (above). He and his wife clipped a small gift to each of the twenty-four clothespins, including a screwdriver set, apple corer, pin punches, thumb tacks, and a meat tenderizer. Students may similarly each select a small gift and offer them creatively to a teacher who is marrying. **TOP:** CHRISTY KAUFFMAN, **BOTTOM:** BETH OBERHOLTZER

When her younger brother got married, Katie and her husband, along with her other married siblings, bought a wheelbarrow for the couple. Each of the groom's fourteen nieces and nephews selected a new toy to wrap and place in the barrow: a baby doll, a small horse, a stuffed bunny, a bat and ball, the game Memory, and several board games. Jay and Rose received a children's wagon and a laundry cart filled with toys from their nieces and nephews from both sides of the family. The toys were not for the baby the children's uncle and aunt would likely have—they were something for the children themselves to play with when they visited.

Traditionally, the gifts that were brought to the wedding were collected and displayed in the bride's bedroom. Immediate family usually gave "on the bed" gifts, and other guests would give gifts when the couple visited them in the months after the wedding. After dinner, the couple and the bride's friends would gather in the bedroom to open the gifts.

When Moses and Susie married in 1968, the ten or twenty gifts brought to the wedding—by close family or guests who traveled a long distance to be there and by English guests—were arranged for display on the bride's bed. "And the bed wasn't even covered," Susie recalled. In the late fall and winter after their wedding, Moses and Susie paid a series of visits—sometimes two or three in one day—to all the guests who had attended their wedding. Their social time for months, often from Friday evening through Monday evening, consisted of paying calls on family. They had a chance to share a meal and play games with the children—sometimes staying the night—and receive their wedding gifts.

When Gideon and Leah married in 2009, they received several dozen gifts at the wedding and displayed and opened them in a spare bedroom. They made a good number of post-wedding visits, but at a somewhat leisurely pace, and mostly to relatives nearby.

Amos, who runs his own business, cleverly manages the when-to-give-the-gift puzzle. He might give a hand tool set to a worker at the employee's wedding. Then, when the newlyweds visit his family, he gives an additional tool that fits in the set.

Since the trend has moved toward more guests bringing gifts to the wedding rather than giving them at subsequent visits, the gift collection is set up in a dedicated public area. Attendants collect the gifts when guests arrive and carry them to specially set up display tables. Though the dinner tables in the wedding room have limited decoration, the gift area is enlivened with flowers, candles, ribbons, and displays of names and scripture verses.

Opening the gifts is no longer just for the groom, the bride, and her buddy girls. Today, a couple and their side sitters open gifts while gathered family and friends sing to them in the family's recreation room.

Visiting and singings

One of Rose's favorite parts of gathering with her youth group was the singing. She and her new husband Jay experienced that sweetness one more time after their wedding dinner when guests gathered and sang

Directly after the newlyweds and young people finish their noon meal, they will gather in this rec room. The couple and their side sitters stand in front of the display and open their gifts while friends and relatives sing. **TOP:** BETH OBERHOLTZER, **LEFT:** CHRISTY KAUFFMAN

gospel songs—in English and in parts—for a little over an hour while they opened gifts. Rose had created her own playlist by selecting sixteen songs and collecting the music into a custom booklet. The impromptu chorus consisted of their friends, standing along the sides and at the back of the room. Parents and grandparents settled into chairs at the front, sometimes joining in with the younger voices raised high in praise to God.

While the singing and gift-opening is taking place, dinner is served to people at the second and third seatings in the wedding room.

Some youth skip the gift-opening and singing and head right outside to play volleyball or other games. The rest of the youth join in the games and socializing after the gifts are opened. Traditionally, the bride and groom would separate to enjoy time with their same-gender friends; the groom and his side sitters would pass out beef sticks and candy to friends while the bride's side sitters offered treats from baskets they carried. More modern newlyweds stay together to spend time with friends. In addition to the handouts, there is often a display with a variety of candies for guests to help themselves.

"I like to check where my horse is during the day; if it was moved, it would be hard to find in the dark."

When the bride and groom briefly parted to be with their friends on the afternoon of Steven's wedding some years ago, he packed the pockets of his wedding suit with beef sticks, candy, and gum. His two side sitters did the same. Friends approached and kidded with him: "What do you have in those pockets?" He passed out the beef sticks. "What else do you have?" He passed out Mentos and Starbursts, then headed to the house for a refill. Mindful of the day's demands on the groom, many friends would approach the side sitters instead with their treat requests.

Married folks welcome time in the afternoon to catch up with friends. Paper ladies take a break from intensive food management to visit a bit also, but they still make sure that the ongoing tasks of cleaning and maintenance are done. Men often look in on their horses midday, partly to make sure all is well and partly to make sure they know where the horses are.

Eck tenders may be called on to help in the afternoon, perhaps preparing a tasty punch to serve to the *yunges* or distributing wedding favors.

Words and Tunes

Singing is integral to faith and community for the Amish. Four times are set aside for mostly German-language singing throughout the traditional fourteen-hour wedding day. The language, tempo, and whether sung in unison or parts depend on the occasion, the book used, and the tune selected. There is no accompaniment.

- **At the beginning and end of the church service:** Singing is in German from the *Ausbund*; voices are in unison; the tempo is slow.
- **While the bride and groom open their gifts:** The singing of a variety of gospel selections is in English; voices are in four-part harmony; the tempo is fast.
- **Afternoon:** Singing is in German from the *Ausbund*; voices are in unison; the tempo for some songs is slow and some fast, depending on the tune.
- **Evening:** Singing is from the *Gesangbuch* in German, voices are in unison; the tempo is fast.

One popular gift for friends of the bridal couple is glass mugs etched with the names of the couple and filled with a signature beverage such as non-alcoholic spritzers or kombucha. Some hosts set up a coffee bar or a candy table for guests to choose a drink or a sweet.

The Forgeher are keeping an eye on the clock, and as three o'clock nears, they rearrange chairs and benches for the afternoon singing in the wedding room. If some of the *yunges* are slow to come in, the Forgeher may need to take a walk around the property and issue reminders that it's time to come together.

The young people sit at the Big Table while other folks sit on rows of chairs and benches in the middle of the room. The bridal couple's fathers, grandfathers, and uncles sit in the first row of chairs with the mothers, grandmothers, and aunts immediately behind them in the second row of chairs. Filling in the remaining rows of chairs, then benches, are any additional uncles, aunts, and married siblings and in-laws—in order of age and relationship to the couple—in alternating rows of men and women. More distant relatives and church people are seated toward the back. Ministers and bishops, with their wives, are seated according to their age and relationship to the bride or groom rather than their status in the church.

Traditionally, single guys, one at a time, would approach the group of single young women and invite one to go to the singing with him. The gathered young women simply waited to be asked. (Refusing an invitation wasn't likely.) When single women are younger and popular and outgoing, it's fun. If they're shy or quiet or older, it's stressful.

Instead, some recent brides have the young men and women line up in the order in which they entered the morning service and then pair off as the two lines meet. Couples who are dating or engaged are automatically paired together. Susie, eighty-four, lamented the end of the boy-picks-girl tradition. However, she did admit that she was always one of the girls chosen early on.

Since the young people go in as couples in the afternoon and evening, young men and women sit together on the same side of the table rather than facing each other across the table.

The afternoon singing is also called "afternoon table," and the snacks are often the equivalent of an entire meal. The bride's uncles have set each singer's place at the table with a small plate, a cup of water, and a cup of punch. They place one of the cakes given as a gift in front of the newlyweds.

A generation ago, a couple may have received ten or more cakes as Eck gifts. Since fewer gift cakes are brought these days, the Eck tenders make sure there is at least one. The ceremonial cake cutting takes place after everyone is seated at the afternoon table. The bride and groom grip the knife together and cut a wedge of cake, then carefully work together to lay the piece on its side on top of the cake. Two generations ago, the bride would have cut the cake without the groom's help, but popular culture influence has led to the partnership and occasionally some mild cake shenanigans. The cake is not served at this time. Depending how many cakes are received, this one may be cut and served at supper—or saved for the *Infehr* (later reception).

An array of finger foods is passed around during the singing to keep up the participants' strength and spirits. The spread may include potato chips, little sausages, soft pretzels, vegetables and dip, quesadillas, stuffed mushrooms or peppers wrapped in bacon, or individual desserts. If Eck gifts include platters of meat and cheese, novelty treats, and candy, they are served also. Young siblings and nieces and nephews often stand behind the Eck, ready for any little sweets the honored couple may pass their way.

The bride and groom, who are seated at the Eck, do not join in the singing of hymns in German from the *Ausbund*. Always sung at the start are pages 508, 378, and 712. Four verses of 712 were sung in the morning service; it is continued in the afternoon with verses that reference having a wife. After those three hymns, any of the singers, young woman or young man, can lead out with their chosen hymn and a chosen tune and the others will follow. Depending on the tune selected, the singing could be fast or slow.

Before supper, the hostlers make their last rounds feeding and watering the horses. They perform any farm chores that have been asked—which might include feeding and milking the cows and feeding any other animals. After this, they're off duty for the rest of the evening. When guests leave, each fetches their own horse and hitches it up for the drive home.

Some guests—depending on how close they are to the family, whether they have young children, how far they must go, and whether they have chores waiting for them—head home before the evening meal. If they live close by, they may return after chores are completed. But most guests stay; if there were five hundred guests for dinner, there may be four hundred at supper. Some of the older folks may leave in the afternoon or soon after supper while the younger ones stay to celebrate into the evening.

Going in for supper

As the young people sing in the wedding room, supper preparation is underway in the wedding kitchen. The paper ladies are again overseeing the cooking and the chest ladies are organizing dishes. A new shift of cooks—often six couples who are buddies of the bride's parents—is already in the kitchen, menus at hand, making the evening meal.

Rose and her mother baked lemon cakes to serve at afternoon table and prepared a variety of appetizer-style eats for supper. Rose's parents' buddies, couples in their fifties, will serve as supper cooks. CHRISTY KAUFFMAN

The Forgeher step into the wedding room when the singing wraps up to return the copies of the *Ausbund* to the correct boxes and reconfigure benches and tables as needed for supper. They confirm the supper schedule with the cooks to make sure the series of seatings is timed correctly.

While the young people have a few hours to socialize between the end of the afternoon singing and when they are called in again to eat, the bride and groom have a chance to do a bit of lighthearted matchmaking. They had circulated a clipboard among their single friends and relatives at dinner and asked them to write down their names and whether they would be staying for supper. Referring to that, the newlyweds now make a list of male-female couples that will go in to supper together and attend the evening singing together. At mealtime, Eck tenders announce the names of each couple, who then come forward and are seated beside each other at the table.

Couples who are engaged or dating are automatically put together. Maybe a young man makes a special request about whom he wants to be matched with. Girls are expected to accept whoever comes their way. ("It's only for a few hours!") It is no easy task for the bride and groom to take a list of one hundred *yunges* and pair them up. Some couples are matched with romance in mind; occasionally, couples who never met before hit it off. Some are matched as buddies or cousins. If there is an uneven number of girls or boys, those who haven't been matched simply go in together.

Older folks enjoy looking on to see who has been paired with whom and whether they think it might be a good match. Even so, this is generally viewed as a low-pressure situation, and the participants don't get too exercised about it. Maybe they'll make a new friend.

Beginning at about half past four, the first of three or four seatings for supper takes place at the Family Table. In a reversal of the dinner seating order, the less honored guests eat first. Workers and church people have their meals early, as do supper table waiters and Eck tenders so they can serve guests at the subsequent seatings.

The first seating at the Big Table, at around six o'clock, finds the bride's parents sitting in the Eck. Fanning out beside them and across the table are the groom's parents, the bridal couple's grandparents, the couple's married siblings and in-laws, and close relatives.

Seating for the young people at the Big Table begins at about half past six for the seven o'clock meal. The bridal couple is again seated at the Eck, flanked by their side sitters. The rest of the table is filled with the young people. They are served by young couples who have married within the last year or two.

There is no set menu for supper; the bride and her mother have settled on their favorites like lasagna, salad, and garlic bread or baked chicken, sweet potatoes, and broccoli salad. Fruit salad is popular, followed by perhaps a dessert of apple pie or an apple goody served with ice cream. Eck tenders again serve special treats to just the newlyweds and side sitters.

Evening celebration

For the Forgeher, the last job of the day is reorganizing benches and chairs for the evening singing. The paper ladies, cooks, dishwashers, and other workers clean up and wash dishes. Chest ladies sort and count flatware, dishes, and glasses, then refill the dish chests to be returned the next day. Since there is often a good bit of food left over, several women have the job of making up meals to be delivered to older adults who couldn't attend and packages to go home with the groom's parents or to send to a family with a new baby or a sick family member. The rest of the food goes in the rented portable walk-in cooler.

The evening meal has been a bit more leisurely for the young people since they eat last and don't need to clear out to allow another shift to eat. Their time of eating and socializing segues directly into the evening singing. Still paired as they were for supper, the youth begin their evening singing at about eight. They sing from the *Gesangbuch* in German. Parents, grandparents, and the groom's married aunts, uncles, and siblings—and other married folks—are again seated on the rows of chairs and benches as during the afternoon singing—and join in the singing if they wish.

Though there is still an air of solemnity during the singing, there's a bit more flexibility as the evening goes on. During the singing and before guests begin to leave, some minds turn to mischief. One traditional exploit that is varyingly enjoyed, tolerated, or found a bit worrisome is throwing the groom over the fence. A newly married man's friends may seize him and march him outside to a nearby fence and toss him over, symbolizing his journey from single to married man. In some iterations the groom turns immediately to catch his bride if she is tossed over after him, in others, the bride simply accompanies the group—to, in the words of one sage, "make sure they don't tear him apart."

Lest a guest get a bit hungry or wish for a sweet during the day, it is common for a bride to set up a candy table stocked with a variety of choices. BETH OBERHOLTZER

Jay, carried out by nearly a dozen friends, was the subject of a brief tug-of-war over which fence was better. Care was taken in the toss; he went over feet first and landed safely.

The evening singing for Gideon and his bride went on without major interruption; their youth group—perhaps guided by leaders, parents, and good sense—no longer does the groom-fence thing. They want to maintain the cordial atmosphere of the evening minus the hijinks.

A decade or two ago it was common for friends to trick a bride into stepping over a broom handle, which symbolized that she was now married. Many currently find the reminder unnecessary.

These traditions are more popular and meaningful in some areas than in others. Regardless of whether a tradition is wholeheartedly embraced in a particular community, many parents and grandparents remember and can tell the enthralling details of their own adventures involving grooms and fences.

When guests say farewell to Elam and Mary Ann at the end of the evening, they will be offered a carpenter's pencil or a candle and asked to sign the guest book. BETH OBERHOLTZER

Guests usually say their farewells during the evening singing. The tables have been moved and chairs pushed back to allow space for them to file past the bride and groom to shake their hands. Guests often wish the couple God's blessing, thank them for the invitation to the wedding, and encourage them to visit. The newlyweds hand out favors to each guest and ask them to sign the guest book.

The singing may last until nine or ten at night, largely depending on how much the family enjoys singing and how soon the guests need to leave.

Since the bride and groom spend their first night as a married couple at the bride's home, they are easily available for further teasing. Things have apparently calmed down in the last two or three generations, but stories abound of how friends have pranked the couple on the wedding night: Jonah and Lena's bed was taken apart and reassembled on the porch roof; Ephraim and Verna's buggy was filled with chickens; Elmer and Becky dealt with strange noises outside at all hours of the night; Mervin and Marion had to track down their missing mattress at the far end of a field.

"Despite our differences, we all root for the same cause."

But romance seems to have won out. These days the bride's buddy girls or Eck tenders are much more likely to set a sweet scene than to play tricks. They may scatter rose petals leading up the stairs to the bedroom or place tea lights or candles around the bedroom. They may create a towel sculpture of a pair of intertwined swans and place it on the bed. As one mom said, "That is so much more thoughtful." Even so, the couple is wise to remain alert.

CHRISTY KAUFFMAN

NINE

After the Wedding Day

After the wedding, the bride and groom typically live with her parents for a few months. BETH OBERHOLTZER

The wedding is over, but plenty of related social activities are yet to come. The newlyweds live with the bride's parents in a transition period between the wedding and moving into their own home. When most weddings took place in the fall, the couple waited until spring to move out. Now, since the rhythms of the farm season are less of a guide, the sojourn with parents may only be a few months or sometimes just a few weeks.

Given the massive amount of preparation needed for a wedding, the cleanup and reorganization can be extensive too. The entire family is up early and hard at work the morning after the wedding. The bride and groom clean up the Eck area and finish washing dishes.

Those who helped before and on the day of the wedding descend once again. They disassemble any temporary structures, return rented equipment and appliances, and pack up the bench wagons to be conveyed to their next site. Extra food is organized, and some is sent home with helpers. Eli's eyes lit up when he talked about his duties as an uncle. "When everybody works together, it's a lot of fun," he said.

A traditional early morning day-after chore for the bride and groom is to launder table linens and tea towels and hang them out to dry. In years past this was seen as an invitation to pranks. Friends might have teased the couple by hiding the clothespins, putting fake spiders or a box of horse manure in the washer, or running off with the laundry itself. Pranks are less likely these days. As Katie Ann, a mom of teens and young adults, reminds them, "You have to be sensible."

Transition to married life

Today, young marrieds are more inclined to go on a honeymoon than their parents and grandparents would have been. A romantic getaway may involve a weekend in the mountains or a week at the shore or a trip with or to visit friends.

The bridal couple engages in a series of visits over the next several months to guests who attended their wedding. The number of stops and length of visits varies depending on the couple's preferences, how well the couple knows their hosts, and what is commonly done within their community. The couple might stay for a meal or overnight—or just an hour or two.

All of Melvin's nieces and nephews knew that their wedding gift from him and their aunt would be a handmade seven-foot-long dining room bench—which they would receive when they visited. Some of his nieces and nephews didn't realize that they needed that bench until after they had children, but Uncle Melvin welcomed their visits, however long after the wedding.

At visits, tradition has the groom sharing a game, a joke, a folded-paper trick, or sleight of hand—called "young married tricks"—to entertain the children in the family. Stories abound of amazing feats, one involving a toilet paper tube, a pie plate, an egg, a glass of water, and a broom.

In addition to receiving wedding gifts from the hosts, the couple can enjoy getting to know relatives better, which strengthens their communal ties.

Arlen and Miriam went visiting every weekend and some weeknights in the four months between their December wedding and when they moved into their own home. They managed to visit everyone who came to

When operating a produce stand, a couple may work together planting and tending the vegetables. In the spring and summer, the husband does most of the field work while the wife prepares the produce to sell and manages the stand. A neighbor girl might be hired to help sell until the couple's children are old enough to take over. DENNIS HUGHES

their wedding, even seeing a guest in West Virginia, and were given gifts at every stop. As Arlen's mother described, "They just plan and visit and plan and visit."

It's not always easy to stay abreast of who's doing what. Or to flex with change. When asked how she knows whether a couple is going to be visiting or whether she should just take a gift to the wedding, sixty-year-old Fanny replied tartly, "I have the gift. If they don't visit, they don't get it."

Jay and Rose received most of their gifts on their wedding day, so their visits after the wedding were primarily to close family. During their time of relative freedom while living with Rose's family, they talked happily about their ten-day trip to Florida in December. It was not to relax on the beach but to volunteer with Mennonite Disaster Service repairing homes that were damaged by storms. The change of scenery was welcome—as was the satisfaction that comes from hard work and helping others.

During the time a couple is living with the bride's parents, they attend church with her family. Even though they're married, the new husband goes in (enters the church room) with the boys rather than the married men, and the new wife goes in with the girls rather than the married women. They will go in and sit with their married counterparts—women with women, men with men—when they have moved into their own home and begin attending their own church. Church districts are organized geographically, so a married couple may go to a different church than either of them attended growing up.

Though a beard is commonly known as an indication that an Amish man is married, he does not grow a one before his wedding or immediately after. He grows his beard months later—after the couple moves into their own home and settles into their new church.

Going from single to married is to cross a great divide in the Amish community. Socialization and organization are often based on marital status. Regardless of a married couple's ages compared to single friends, they are met with expectations of maturity and adulthood. A married couple, for example, is put to work at a wedding whereas the unmarried are waited on and indulged at a wedding.

Unmarried young people frolic and play games and hold singings. Upon marriage, a couple focuses on establishing their home. In addition

Beyond Volleyball

Amish young people play a lot of volleyball. They begin in the school-yard and get serious about it at youth group gatherings. That is five or more years of volleyball every Sunday afternoon. They may set up tournaments on religious holidays. Then, abruptly upon marriage, time spent playing volleyball takes a nosedive. Though married people may play very occasionally, it is now considered a sport for the *yunges*. When one young married man was asked whether he missed volleyball, he said, "Not at all. When I go in the house and my baby gives me a big smile, that's what it is now."

to family, their friendships and visits are often with married buddies. Though married folks certainly have fun, there is effort to show a new sobriety in demeanor and thoughtfulness in approach—as in 1 Corinthians 13:11: "When I became a man, I put away childish things."

Infehr

To thank the bride's parents for hosting the wedding and to learn to know their son's new in-laws better, the groom's parents host an *Infehr* (infare, or reception) for the bride's family. The guest list includes members of both sides of the family: parents, grandparents, single and married siblings and in-laws, and the bride and groom's nieces and nephews. The number for the dinner and nearly daylong visit can easily reach sixty or more.

The *Infehr* is usually held within a few months of the wedding, but could occur up to a year after. Some like to host in warm weather so it can take place outside. Fanny likes to host inside; then everyone is together visiting. She said, "If we're outside, the men go out to the barn to talk among themselves. If we're inside in the winter, everyone visits together."

There is no set menu, though the bride's family usually brings a cake that was a gift at the wedding and has been frozen for this occasion. The cake at Arlen and Miriam's *Infehr* was a gift from Reuben, Arlen's brother, who was a side sitter at the wedding.

Going forward: At home and at work

Moving into their own place after spending some months living with the bride's family is a big step for the newlyweds. The new home may be a rental or a family-supported purchase, but it is certainly within an Amish community.

Many farms and properties are home to several generations of one family. A young couple in their early twenties may move into an addition to the main house or a small house on the property of his or her parents, who might be in their forties or fifties. As the younger couple adds children to the family, the older couple may no longer need as much space, and the two families switch. The older couple moves to the smaller quarters and the young couple can spread out in the larger house with their expanding family. An elderly grandparent or other relative may also live in a small house or apartment on the property.

Thanks to the generosity of their parents, the couple has all the furniture and most of the household goods they need. They now work together to make a home—in some ways common to couples everywhere, in other ways unique to their community. They will settle their horse into its new stall and stock up on feed and bedding, rework the existing garden plot or make a new one, and map out transportation to work if needed.

Prior to marriage, a young man will have considered whether he wants to continue the work he was doing in his teens and early twenties as his "married job." If he works on the farm, can the family farm support him, or does he need to be looking for his own farm? If working in a trade, are his skills in high demand, is advancement possible, can he become his own boss? He now has a wife, and soon will likely have children to provide for.

Lavina enjoyed working with the draft horses when she was growing up and now partners with her husband at harvesttime. When the children are older, they will also help. JOHN HERR

Many Amish couples welcome their first child within the first year or two of marriage and go on to have seven or eight children over the next twenty or so years. Sometimes, if a couple is not blessed with biological children, they grow especially close to nieces and nephews. Less often, they work through a local social service agency to adopt. Children, however they arrive, are a blessing that helps ensure continuation of family and community.

Young women who marry are expected to—and want to—prioritize taking care of their homes and families. If a couple lives on a farm, the work is a partnership. Women often drive teams in the field for planting and harvest, especially before a couple's children are old enough to help. Women are adept at integrating generating income with their other duties. Sometimes, it's just a little extra cash. Other times it's more: a cut-flower stand at the end of the lane becomes a bloom-packed market stand, the plethora of cucumbers in the garden become seven kinds of pickles to sell at a city farm market, or routine sewing for the family becomes custom work for an Amish clothing shop.

In farm families, it is quite common for nearly grown sons to take over a portion of the farming. For example, the son may take the lead when growing and tending the tobacco while Dad continues with the milking and growing fodder crops. With multiple sons, or no sons, it can be a puzzle to work out who should take over the farm when Dad is ready to slow down.

Farming Transition

Through his childhood and youth, Arlen worked on his family's dairy and crop farm. When he left formal schooling at fifteen, he began working away from home as a carpenter while continuing to help on the farm.

The year before he got married, Arlen and his parents had a talk. Did Arlen want to be a carpenter all his life or "farm and stay home more"? He chose farming. Both of his older brothers were established in their work, and neither was interested in taking over the dairy farm when their dad, at sixty, was ready to slow down. The timing aligned nicely. The two of them planned it out carefully. Arlen would take over the dairy cows and main crops of hay and corn while his dad grew wheat (and gave the straw to Arlen to bed the cows). Dad would help with planting and harvesting, in whatever way he could. They each would farm a four-acre plot of tobacco. Miriam, Arlen's intended, grew up in a family with milk cows and a cheese business, so she was accustomed to the work of a dairy farm.

Three years into Arlen and Miriam's marriage, the labor division is working. Arlen and Miriam find the hard work a challenge, but she said, "He has never come home and said he doesn't want to do it." Recently, when Arlen headed to the barn to milk after an early supper, Miriam went out to help. They took five-month-old Becca along to nap in her stroller in the barn.

On a Tuesday evening in late October, Jay and Rose sat together at the Eck and breathed a deep sigh. They felt giddy relief ("Yay! We're married!") alongside a deep contentment. The room was packed with relatives and friends; all these people were there to celebrate their marriage and support them on their journey. The day had been a happy blur, and now their guests were lined up to say goodbye. It was over . . . but just starting.

CHRISTY KAUFFMAN

Notes

1. Mennonite Disaster Service estimate (phone conversation with Brad Fair, MDS Development Manager, August 29, 2023).

2. Jeff Hawkes, "Amish Population Grows by 1,000 a Year, Despite Lancaster County's Urban Sprawl, Development," *LNP*, May 19, 2019, https://lancasteronline.com/news/local/amish-population-grows-by-a-year-despite-lancaster-county-s/article_e24c564e-678e-11e9-9ba4-bf1905bae642.html; "Twelve Largest Amish Settlements, 2023," Young Center for Anabaptist and Pietist Studies, Elizabethtown College, http://groups.etown.edu/amishstudies/statistics/twelve-largest-settlements-2023/.

3. Sam S. Stoltzfus, *What It's Like to Be Amish* (Walnut Street Books, 2018), 105.

4. Stoltzfus, 105–6.

5. Joseph F. Donnermeyer, "A Demographic Profile of the Greater Lancaster County, Pennsylvania, Amish," *Journal of Plain Anabaptist Communities* 3, no. 2 (May 30, 2023), https://doi.org/10.18061/jpac.v3i2.9154.

6. Stoltzfus, *What It's Like to Be Amish*, 105.

7. Shunning is a ritual practiced by the Amish that is outside the parameters of this book. Author Steven M. Nolt defines shunning as "the ritualized recognition that a relationship has been broken and that things will not be the same unless the relationship is righted" (*The Amish: A Concise Introduction*, Johns Hopkins Press, 2016, 50). Also refer to Donald B. Kraybill, Steven M. Nolt, and David L. Weaver-Zercher, *The Amish Way: Patient Faith in a Perilous World* (Jossey-Bass, 2010), or Donald B. Kraybill, *The Riddle of the Amish Culture* (Johns Hopkins Press, 2001).

Andrew (top left) and Kathleen (top right) help with their family's draft horses during field demonstrations. Christian (above) drives his own team. BETH OBERHOLTZER

Further Reading

JOHN HERR

1001 Questions and Answers on the Christian Life (Pathway Publishing Corp., 1992).

Fisher, Barbie, *As Two Become One* (Dillwyn, VA, 2020, 434-414-8222).

Glick, Susan Marie, *The Ultimate Wedding Planner* (Loysville, PA, 2021, 717-636-2354).

Johnson-Weiner, Karen M., *The Lives of Amish Women* (Johns Hopkins University Press, 2013).

Kraybill, Donald B., Karen M. Johnson-Weiner, and Steven M. Nolt, *The Amish* (Johns Hopkins University Press, 2013).

Kraybill, Donald B., *What the Amish Teach Us: Plain Living in a Busy World* (Johns Hopkins University Press, 2021).

Scott, Stephen, *The Amish Wedding: And Other Special Occasions of the Old Order Communities* (Good Books, 1988).

Stevick, Richard A., *Growing Up Amish: The Rumspringa Years* (Johns Hopkins University Press, 2014).

Stoltzfus, Sam S., *What It's Like to Be Amish: Reflections of an Amish Farmer* (Walnut Street Books, 2018).

Wesner, Erik J., "Marriage," Amish America, February 17, 2015, amishamerica.com/marriage/.

JOHN HERR

The Author

Beth Oberholtzer is an author and book designer from Lancaster, Pennsylvania. She grew up in a Mennonite family on a farm in Lancaster County. Her books explore aspects of Old Order life in Lancaster County, and include *Plain Meetinghouses, Working Horses,* and *Amish Gardens.* She has also written and photographed several craft books and designed hundreds of books for a variety of publishing clients.